About Haecceity

This book offers an in-depth and updated examination of the nature of haecceity—that primitive entity which explains why something is distinct from other things.

This book begins by exploring different conceptions of haecceity throughout history. The discussion of various figures across history is important for getting clear on the nature of haecceity and its role in individuation. The next part of this book examines different views about the nature of haecceity. The author defends a view on which haecceities have objects that instantiate them as constituents. Following that, this book considers arguments for and against the existence of haecceities, the epistemology of haecceity, and the distinction between qualitative and non-qualitative properties.

About Haecceity will appeal to scholars and advanced students working in metaphysics, philosophy of language, epistemology, logic, and history of philosophy.

Matthew Davidson is Professor and Chair of Philosophy at California State University, San Bernardino. He works in metaphysics, philosophy of religion, and philosophy of language. His recent publications include *The Metaphysics of Existence and Nonexistence* and *Knowledge and Reality in Nine Questions*.

Routledge Studies in Metaphysics

Death, Determinism, and Meaning
Stephen Maitzen

A Case for Necessitarianism
Amy Karofsky

E.J. Lowe and Ontology
Edited by Miroslaw Szatkowski

A Map of Selves
Beyond Philosophy of Mind
N. M. L. Nathan

Meaning and Metaphysical Necessity
Tristan Grøtvedt Haze

Relational Passage of Time
Matias Slavov

Political Identity and the Metaphysics of Polities
Edited by Gabriele De Anna and Manuele Dozzi

Powers, Parts and Wholes
Essays on the Mereology of Powers
Edited by Christopher J. Austin, Anna Marmodoro, and Andrea Roselli

About Haecceity
An Essay in Ontology
Matthew Davidson

For more information about this series, please visit: https://www.routledge.com/Routledge-Studies-in-Metaphysics/book-series/RSM

About Haecceity
An Essay in Ontology

Matthew Davidson

NEW YORK AND LONDON

First published 2024
by Routledge
605 Third Avenue, New York, NY 10158

and by Routledge
4 Park Square, Milton Park, Abingdon, Oxon, OX14 4RN

Routledge is an imprint of the Taylor & Francis Group, an informa business

© 2024 Matthew Davidson

The right of Matthew Davidson to be identified as author of this work has been asserted in accordance with sections 77 and 78 of the Copyright, Designs and Patents Act 1988.

All rights reserved. No part of this book may be reprinted or reproduced or utilised in any form or by any electronic, mechanical, or other means, now known or hereafter invented, including photocopying and recording, or in any information storage or retrieval system, without permission in writing from the publishers.

Trademark notice: Product or corporate names may be trademarks or registered trademarks, and are used only for identification and explanation without intent to infringe.

ISBN: 978-1-032-57514-8 (hbk)
ISBN: 978-1-032-57516-2 (pbk)
ISBN: 978-1-003-43973-8 (ebk)

DOI: 10.4324/9781003439738

Typeset in Sabon
by codeMantra

For Mom and Umma

Contents

    Preface   ix

    Introduction   1

1 Preliminaries: Haecceity Through History   5
   1.1 *John Duns Scotus* 6
   1.2 *William of Ockham* 10
   1.3 *Francisco Suárez* 12
   1.4 *G.W. Leibniz* 14
   1.5 *C.S. Peirce* 18
   1.6 *Alvin Plantinga* 20
   1.7 *Roderick Chisholm* 21
   1.8 *Robert Adams* 23
   1.9 *Gary Rosenkrantz* 24
   1.10 *Conclusion* 25

2 The Nature of Haecceity   28
   2.1 *Three Types of Haecceity: Some Statements* 28
   2.2 *An Assessment of the Different Views of Haecceity* 31

3 Haecceity: Arguments for and Against   43
   3.1 *Arguments for Haecceity* 43
   3.2 *Arguments against Haecceity* 64

4 Qualitative and Quidditative Properties   74
   4.1 *The Qualitative/Quidditative Distinction Intuitively Characterized* 74
   4.2 *The Linguistic View* 75
   4.3 *The Entailment View* 76
   4.4 *The Dependence View* 77
   4.5 *The Relational View* 79
   4.6 *Quidditative Constituentism* 83

viii *Contents*

5 **Haecceity and Existence**   86
   5.1 Arguments that Haecceities Don't Depend for Their Existence on the Objects that Instantiate Them 86
   5.2 Arguments that Haecceities Depend for Their Existence on the Objects that Instantiate Them 95

6 **Haecceity and Acquaintance**   100
   6.1 Concerning Acquaintance with Haecceities 100
   6.2 A Kvanvigian Argument against "The Haecceity Theory" 102
   6.3 The Argument from Reidentification 104

7 **Haecceity Applied: Thisness Presentism**   109
   7.1 Application 1: Complete Singular Propositions 109
   7.2 Application 2: Presentism and Grounding Past Truths 115
   7.3 Application 3: Presentism and Passage 120

Epilogue   *129*
Bibliography   *131*
Index   *141*

Preface

Thanks to Ed Wierenga and Jim Van Cleve for very helpful comments on the entirety of the manuscript. Thanks to Vera Hoffman-Kolss for discussion of quidditative properties, and Chris Menzel for discussion of various issues in the text. Thanks to three anonymous reviewers for Routledge who made the book better with their suggestions.

Introduction

This is a book about haecceity.[1] There are a few well-known (at least among philosophers working in a particular vein of metaphysics) arguments for the existence of haecceities that we find in places like Robert Adams' seminal "Primitive Thisness and Primitive Identity" or Gary Rosenkrantz's *Haecceity: An Ontological Essay*. But there has been a notable dearth of material about what sort of thing haecceity is. One of my main aims in this book is to investigate the nature of haecceity. I hope my efforts here will prove of some use to those who seek to understand the logical space of views around the nature of haecceity.

This book isn't just about what haecceities are, however. I also consider arguments for and against the existence of haecceities, the epistemology of haecceity, the nature of qualitative and quidditative properties, and ways one may use haecceities in bolstering a metaphysical theory. Thus, it does contain the sorts of topics that one finds in previous work on haecceities, though the positions I take on them are almost entirely novel.

This book comprises seven chapters. In Chapter 1, I explore different conceptions of haecceity throughout history, from Scotus in the late 13th and early 14th centuries to Gary Rosenkrantz in the late 20th century. We have a general functional conception of haecceity with which we will operate in this book: an haecceity of an object x is that entity which explains the entelechy or thingness of x, and/or explains x's distinctness from all other objects. Beyond this general functional conception, however, one might have thought that there was through history a more-or-less uniform conception of the sort of thing haecceity is. This turns out not to be the case. It is striking to see how much different figures through history disagree about the nature of haecceity. (Some of what I argue in this book adds to the disagreement.) This history also contains important criticisms of haecceity that shed light on the proper role of haecceity in individuation.

DOI: 10.4324/9781003439738-1

2 Introduction

I use the different conceptions of haecceity one finds in Chapter 1 to inform Chapter 2, which is on the nature of haecceity. There I consider three general sorts of views about haecceity, namely, partism, primitivism, and constituentism. The *partist* about haecceity thinks that haecceities are parts—in some robust sense of "part"—of objects. Scotus himself is a partist; he thinks that haecceities are parts of substantial forms. The *primitivist* about haecceity thinks that haecceities are properties that are primitive in their structure. Most contemporary defenders of haecceities are primitivists. The *constituentist* thinks that haecceities are properties that have as constituents the objects that exemplify them. I consider different flavors of the three general sorts of views throughout the course of the chapter. I defend a species of constituentism, *sui generis* constituentism. The *sui generis* constituentist thinks that an haecceity has as an element a *sui generis* abstract object. I argue that it has advantages over the other constituentist view, slot-theoretic constituentism; that constituentism is to be preferred over primitivism; and that constituentism and primitivism are to be preferred over partism.

In Chapter 3, I consider arguments for and against the existence of haecceities. There are two sorts of arguments for the existence of haecceities that I take up, namely, *individuative* and *semantic* arguments. Individuative arguments for haecceities posit haecceity to explain the thingness of an entity or to explain how an entity x is distinct from an entity y. The classic arguments for the existence of haecceities that one finds in places like Adams' "Primitive Thisness and Primitive Identity" and Rosenkrantz's *Haecceity: An Ontological Essay* are individuative arguments. Semantic arguments for haecceity posit haecceities to provide semantic values for linguistic expressions (like predicates) or truth conditions for modal sentences. I argue that individuative arguments for haecceities fail, as they do not show that individuation requires haecceities. However, I argue that there are good semantic arguments for haecceities. Thus, we have a *prima facie* reason for thinking that there are haecceities.

In the second half of Chapter 3, I consider a number of arguments against the existence of haecceities. I argue that none is successful in showing that there can't be haecceities. Thus, the overall conclusion of Chapter 3 is that we have reason to think that there are haecceities.

In Chapter 4, I take up the distinction between qualitative and nonqualitative (which I call "quidditative") properties. I consider a number of different accounts of the difference. These include (i) the linguistic view, on which a property is quidditative because it is expressed by a linguistic item with a rigid term in it; (ii) the entailment view, on which a property is quidditative because its instantiation entails the existence of an object beyond the instantiator; (iii) the dependence view, on which a property is quidditative because its existence depends on the existence of some other object; and (iv) the relational view, on which a property is quidditative because its instantiation entails the holding of a relation between the instantiator and some other object. I argue that all of these views fail. I defend a view that I call *quidditative constituentism*, on which a property is quidditative if it has an object as a constituent. Thus, *being taller than Socrates* is quidditative because it has Socrates as a constituent. I argue that quidditative constituentism is superior to the other extant views as an account of the qualitative/quidditative distinction.

In Chapter 5, I consider the question of whether haecceities are dependent for their existence on objects that instantiate them. I consider a number of arguments that there can be unexemplified haecceities, including the argument that they are necessary for giving actualist truth conditions for modal sentences. I also consider a number of arguments against the possibility of unexemplified haecceities. I argue that some of the arguments for unexemplified haecceities are successful, while none of the arguments against unexemplified haecceities is. Thus, I conclude we have reason to think there are unexemplified haecceities.

In Chapter 6, I ask the question: which haecceities are we acquainted with? There have been arguments that we are not able to grasp haecceities of ordinary objects in our environment. I consider in Chapter 6 the best-developed argument from Gary Rosenkrantz's *Haecceity: An Ontological Essay*. I argue that it fails to show that we cannot grasp haecceities of ordinary objects in our environment. I also argue that the constituentist has a ready account of how we grasp haecceities of objects around us. Having earlier defended constituentism, I conclude that we are able to grasp a wide class of haecceities and that the class is far wider than philosophers like Gary Rosenkrantz and Roderick Chisholm have insisted.

In Chapter 7, I consider a recent work from David Ingram (Ingram [69, 70, 71]) in which he uses haecceities to address problems encountered by presentists in the metaphysics of time. Ingram calls his view *Thisness Presentism*. He argues that it offers novel, successful replies to problems of propositional constituency, grounding, and temporal passage. I argue that his Thisness Presentistic solutions to these problems are not successful. Nevertheless, they do show an interesting and wide-ranging recent attempt to use haecceities to solve problems that arise in the philosophy of time.

Note

1 I note upfront that this book is not about *haecceitism*. Haecceitism is a supervenience claim; roughly, it is the claim that there can be quidditative or non-qualitative differences between worlds without having qualitative differences

between them. One might think to appeal to haecceities as a way to explain why haecceitism holds. But the existence of haecceities is neither necessary nor sufficient for the truth of haecceitism. One might hold there are haecceities and deny that there can be merely quidditative differences between worlds. Or, one might think that there can be merely quidditative differences between worlds without thinking that these differences are grounded in the existence of haecceities. We take up issues related to this last point in Chapter 2.

1 Preliminaries
Haecceity Through History

In this first chapter, I want to set the stage for further theorizing about haecceity by considering some of the different views of haecceity that have been held by various figures throughout history. The history we will cover here runs from John Duns Scotus in the late 13th and early 14th centuries to Gary Rosenkrantz at the end of the 20th century. Obviously, there isn't the space in a single chapter to write about everyone who has had something to say about haecceities during that span of time. Thus, I've chosen representative philosophers whose theorizing is particularly important for understanding the development of thinking around haecceity and individuation. Many of these philosophers are well known for having something to say about haecceity (e.g., Scotus and Robert Adams), though not all are (Leibniz and C.S. Peirce). With respect to these figures, I have tried to help the reader see the general outlines of what each has said about haecceity and how different figures relate and respond to one another across time.

As I mentioned in the Introduction, there is a general functional conception of haecceity that runs from Scotus to Rosenkrantz to the present day: an haecceity of an object x is that entity which explains the entelechy or thingness of x, and/or explains x's distinctness from all other objects. However, as we will see in this chapter, there is significant disagreement among these philosophers as to the *kind* of thing that plays the functional role of haecceity. In particular, we shall see that from Scotus to the early moderns, haecceity is a part of an individual's substantial form. When the concept of haecceity is revived in the 20th century, haecceity has become a property. That this has occurred is perhaps not a surprise. Metaphysicians up to the early 17th century generally were working with a hylomorphic conception of individuals, and individuators would have to conform to a hylomorphic metaphysic. After Descartes and Locke (with Leibniz as an exception to this), philosophers largely abandoned a hylomorphic conception of individual things. However, there still was a role for individuators to play in

DOI: 10.4324/9781003439738-2

metaphysics. It made sense to slot haecceity into the property role as an individuator.

In spite of the change in the conception of the nature of haecceity, there is a dialogue through the centuries between various figures about the existence and nature of haecceity. It will be important for our purposes in this book to have this dialogue before us. We begin with the first person generally thought have coined the term "haecceity," John Duns Scotus.[1]

1.1   John Duns Scotus

Scotus, like other medieval philosophers heavily influenced by Aristotle, thought that material objects were a combination of matter and substantial form. For Scotus, substantial form has, in some robust sense, parts. One of these parts is a *common nature*. Consider then Socrates. Socrates is a composite of substantial form and matter. His substantial form has as a part Socrates' common nature, *humanity*. There was lively debate in the high middle ages about the metaphysical status of common nature. In itself, should we think of it as universal? Particular? Neither? In an influential statement quoted by Scotus, Avicenna said, "Equinity is only equinity. Of itself it is neither one nor several, neither universal nor particular" (Avicenna *Metaphysics* V, Scotus Ord II.3.1.31, p. 63).[2] Scotus thought that Avicenna was right about common nature in thinking that it was neither universal nor particular. If *humanity* were particular, Scotus thought, then there couldn't be multiple individuals who were all of the same type—human. Socrates would not be the same type of creature as Plato. If *humanity* were universal, Scotus thought, then we would be forced to identify all instances of *humanity*; we could not account for the fact that Socrates and Plato are distinct. *Humanity* is, for Scotus, in itself *common*, which is less than universal, though more than particular.

Scotus thought that the common nature could be made universal or particular, though. This is important for Scotus, as there are both many and particular instances of humans. *Humanity* is made universal through the mind, which is just to say that in the case of *humanity*, the concept human is universal. It is more difficult to see how *humanity* is made particular, however. We should begin by getting clear on what we mean for *humanity* to be made particular. In the case of Socrates, there are two questions *vis-à-vis* Socrates' particularity that we can ask. First, how is Socrates distinct from any other human, e.g., Plato? Second, how is it that Socrates is an individual human, an individual human thing?[3] Scotus grounds Socrates' distinctness from other humans and Socrates' individuality by positing the existence of a special sort of entity, an haecceity (though Scotus often uses "individual difference") that makes it the case that the common nature *humanity* in Socrates is particular.

Though haecceity (alongside the common nature) is a part of the substantial form, the haecceity for Scotus has no parts and more generally no hylomorphic structure.[4] If it had either, we would have a new problem of individuation for the haecceity. It is, in some sense, intrinsically individual (*de se hoc*) and is capable of lending its individuality to the common nature. We are told very little that is informative about the haecceity itself. As Peter King puts it, "Scotus seems to treat the [haecceity] as a theoretical black box: a given [haecceity] is that which produces a given individual from an uncontracted nature, and no more can be said about it" (King [78], p. 59). Scotus calls the haecceity's lending of individuality to the common nature *contracting*. "Singularity belongs to the nature through something [haecceity] in the thing that contracts the nature (Ord II.3.1.1.42, p. 67)." The haecceity causes the common nature and thus substantial form to have the accident of singularity. In the case of Socrates, Socrates' haecceity causes there to be a particular instance of *humanity* in Socrates. This makes it the case that Socrates is an individual and that Socrates is distinct from Plato (who has his own haecceity).

What is the relationship between the nature *humanity* in Socrates and Socrates' haecceity? To answer this question, we begin by noting that medieval philosophers typically acknowledged two sorts of distinctions between things x and y. The first is a *mental* distinction (or distinction of reason), where we can imagine or conceive x existing without y existing; though in reality, x can't exist without y. The second is a *real* distinction, where x and y can exist apart from one another.[5]

Scotus saw a problem when applying these distinctions to a common nature and haecceity. Suppose Socrates' common nature and his haecceity are only mentally distinct. Then, we have trouble making sense of the notion that *humanity* is a *common* nature; it's difficult to see how there can be multiple individuals of the same type—human. Or if we suppose Socrates' common nature and his haecceity are really distinct, then it looks like Socrates has two natures—a common nature and a particular nature. Scotus thought this was implausible.

The Subtle Doctor employs a third distinction intermediate between the first two sorts of distinctions. He calls this a *formal distinction*.[6] We can get the feel of Scotus' formal distinction if we look at its use in theorizing about divine simplicity. Medieval philosophers thought that God was simple; that is, God had no parts. This entailed, they thought, that all of God's attributes were identical. This invites objection: Surely God's omnipotence is distinct from God's omniscience. It is here that Scotus employs his formal distinction. Scotus claims that the attributes of a simple God are formally distinct, so God's omnipotence is formally distinct from God's omniscience. They aren't *really* distinct, as this would contradict divine simplicity. They aren't merely *mentally* distinct; rather, there is something outside of our minds and in the nature of God that grounds a distinction between the two attributes. They are more than mentally distinct, yet less than really distinct. Scotus uses his third sort of distinction to try explain the relationship between Socrates' common nature *humanity* and Socrates' haecceity: The two are formally distinct.[7]

Scotus argues for the necessity of haecceity by considering and rejecting other accounts of individuality. I want to call attention to three of the views that he rejects, as his reasoning in rejecting them is useful in understanding the intellectual background against which he develops his theory of haecceity.[8]

One competing view of individuation that Scotus argues against is that of Henry of Ghent (Ord. II.3.1.2, pp. 68 ff.). Henry claimed that substances were individuated by "double negation." He thought that we have an individual x if we have something over and above x's parts (so x is not its parts—negation 1) and if x is distinct from everything else (so x is not anything else—negation 2). To this proposal, Scotus objects that the fact that something is not its parts or is distinct from everything else presupposes individuality and thus can't be used to explain individuality. He also points out that Socrates and Plato both are distinct from everything else and are over and above their parts, so on Henry's theory we should identify them. (If one is tempted to reply that Socrates is over and above *these* parts and is distinct from everything else *including Plato*, Scotus' first objection has even more bite.)

Another competing view of individuation that Scotus argues against is individuation by matter (Ord. II.3.1.5–6, pp. 93 ff.). This is famously a theory set out by Aristotle. Scotus cites various passages in Aristotle that suggest such a theory, including from *Metaphysics* VII.8 1034a 5–9:

> And when we have the whole, such and such a form in this flesh in in these bones, this is Callias or Socrates; and they are different in virtue of their matter (for that is different), but the same in form, for their form is indivisible (Ord. II.3.1.5–6, p. 94).

Scotus argues that matter cannot be the basis of individuation. Socrates and Plato both are composites of substantial form and matter, yet are distinct. We might be tempted to try to single out the matter with Socrates' accidents to distinguish it from the matter with Plato's accidents. Scotus argues that distinguishing *these* accidents from *those* accidents presupposes individuality on the part of the substances that have them (Ord II.3.1.4.99, p. 83; see Bates [13] p. 103 for further discussion).

A third account of individuality that Scotus considers is that things are self-individuating (Ord II.3.1.q1, pp. 57 ff.). As we shall see, this (put generally) is the view of Ockham, and it is a view that will loom large in our discussion of individuation in this book. Scotus imagines the self-individuating view to involve a nature that is itself self-individuating. Scotus thinks that we would not be able to account for our ability to know objects have features in common if the nature were self-individuating. The existence of a nature common between Plato and Socrates has an epistemological motivation for Scotus; it is because we grasp the same nature in each of them that we may know they are of the same type.[9]

Let's take stock of Scotus' views concerning individuation. Scotus begins with medieval hylomorphic metaphysic of material objects and less-than-universal (though still common) conception of natures, which is inspired by that of Avicenna. From these, he argues that one is left with a problem of individuation for material objects, and this problem may be solved only by adding an additional part—haecceity—to the substantial form of the material object. The haecceity causes (by contracting) the common nature to be particular. In the case of Socrates, Socrates' haecceity causes Socrates' *humanity* to be individual to Socrates. This makes it the case that Socrates is an individual human and is distinct from all other humans.

1.1.1   Some Questions for Scotus

As in subsequent sections of the chapter, we move to those who react to Scotus' theorizing about haecceity; it is worth stopping here to pose a few questions for Scotus. Some of these are questions I myself have for Scotus. Some of these (and there is an overlap from the first category) are questions that metaphysicians reacting to Scotus have asked of Scotus.

1 Scotus has already backed off from thinking of natures as universals. Natures are common, though not universals. So, this is a lower-grade realism about natures than one finds in some other medieval philosophers. Why isn't such a lower-grade realism consistent with the nature being particular? Could its realism be further reduced to where the nature could be both common and self-individuating?[10]

2 Why do we need to add something which is primitively individuating to the form to get the form to be a particular form? Couldn't the primitive be located not in an additional entity, but in the overall form itself? Isn't this preferable to adding an additional element to the form about which we can say only that it is self-individuating and makes the form individual?

3 Why do we need the nature to be common at all? Scotus already has adopted a lower-grade realism in conceiving of natures as common, though not universal. Why not just think of the nature as particular? If each nature is particular to begin with, there is no need to make it so.

4 If we do think of the nature as particular, why not think that there really is no common nature in reality at all? Why not say that we merely think and talk as though there are common natures?

5 Why do we need a hylomorphic metaphysic at all? Why not dispense with substantial forms altogether?

Were this a book on general scholastic metaphysics, we could pursue answers to all of these questions. This is not such a book. But I think that it is important at least to note these questions. This is for two reasons. First, noting them helps us in assessing Scotus' theorizing around the existence and nature of haecceity. Second, it is instructive to see how subsequent thinkers address these questions. We will see that in response to the questions in (3), Ockham, Suárez, and Leibniz think we should deny that the nature is common at all. We will see that there are claims in Suárez that hint at adopting the strategy suggested by the questions in (2). We also will see, in response to the questions in (4), that Ockham and Leibniz (and perhaps Suárez) think that we should say that talk and thought of common natures doesn't correspond to anything real in the world. Last, we also will see in response to the questions in (5) that 20th century believers in haecceity dispense completely with a form-matter ontology.

We turn to two medieval philosophers who launched important criticisms of Scotus' idea of haecceity, namely, Ockham and Suárez.

1.2   William of Ockham

Ockham read Scotus carefully and was heavily influenced by Scotus' discussion of individuation. At the outset of his criticism of Scotus in the *Ordinatio*, Ockham gives a clear statement of Scotus' view. We get the sense from the care with which he presents Scotus' claims that he has a great deal of respect for Scotus [who, in Ockham's estimation, "surpasses all others in the subtlety of his judgment" (Ord. d2.q6.6, p. 153)] and wants to make sure that there is no straw-manning of Scotus' position on individuation.[11] Here is the main section of his statement of Scotus' view concerning haecceity:

> [I]t is said [by Scotus] that in a thing outside the soul there is a nature really the same as a difference [the haecceity] that contracts it to a determinate individual, and yet formally distinct from that difference. The nature is of itself neither universal nor particular. Rather it is incompletely universal in the thing, and completely universal according to the being it has in the intellect.
>
> [T]his theory maintains that the nature is not *of itself* a this, but through something added...

> [W]ith respect to the contracting difference, this theory claims: First, the individual difference is not quidditative. Second the nature is naturally prior to this contracting difference. Third, the opposite of this individual difference–that is, another individual difference–is not inconsistent with the nature of itself, just as this individual difference does not belong to it of itself...Likewise, the individual difference and the nature are not distinguished as one thing and another thing...they are distinguished only formally (Ord d2.q6.6–9, pp. 153-154).[12]

Ockham clearly states Scotus' theory so as to proceed in rejecting it. Indeed, Ockham's conclusions about individuation are very different from those of Scotus. Scotus maintains some sort of realism about common natures and as a result feels compelled to posit the existence of haecceity to account for the individuality of distinct individuals who share the same common nature. Ockham rejects any sort of realism about common natures. Socrates and Plato don't share a common nature, though we do choose to talk as though they do. Universals, to the extent there are such things, are names or mental items. Ockham gives a number of arguments against various realisms about universals, from Scotus' "moderate realism" to full-blown Platonism.[13] These arguments are intricate and involved.[14] For our purposes here, we may note that Ockham's principal reason for rejecting these various sorts of realisms about natures is that he thinks he can do the metaphysical work he wants to do without real common or universal natures. Thus, there is no need to posit their existence. He wields his razor.

As there is no common nature shared between Socrates and Plato, Ockham feels no pressure to posit an haecceity to explain what makes Socrates distinct from Plato. Rather, Ockham feels that objects are *self-individuating*; that it is a truly primitive fact that *this* is an object and that *this* object is distinct from *that* object. The self-individuation or primitive individuation of objects is a constant theme in his discussion of individuation in the *Ordinatio*. For instance, Ockham says:

> "Singularity immediately pertains to what it belongs to. Therefore, it cannot pertain to it through anything else. Therefore, if something is singular, it is singular by itself (Ord d2.q6.106, p. 171).

He also says:

> "[U]nity does not belong to a nature distinct in any way from individuals. Instead it belongs immediately to the individuals themselves, or (what is the same) to one in comparison with the other" (Ord d2.q6.131, p. 176).

12 Preliminaries

There are many other such passages in the *Ordinatio*.

Ockham rejects Scotus' formal distinction with respect to the difference between haecceity and common nature. He argues that if the common nature can be present in many individuals and the haecceity in only one, it follows via the indiscernibility of identicals that the haecceity and common nature are really and not formally distinct.[15] What Ockham's argument shows, if sound, however, is that haecceity and nature are distinct in the contemporary sense of the term, that is, they are two things. As we noted in the last section, it is not clear whether for Scotus that $x \neq y$ entails that x and y are not formally distinct. But, it does seem clear that $x \neq y$ doesn't entail that x and y are really distinct in Scotus' terminology (i.e., one can exist without the other).

The debate between Scotus and Ockham, generally stated, will be a theme throughout this book. Scotus thinks that for there to be individuation, one needs an extra entity that does the individuation. Ockham contends that individuation is a primitive feature of reality, and it occurs without the mechanism of an additional entity like an haecceity.

1.3   Francisco Suárez

Though he was born nearly two-and-a-half centuries after Scotus died, Suárez, like Ockham before him, was very influenced by Scotus' discussion of individuation. Suárez seems to have held a position between that of Scotus and Ockham. Suárez wasn't a nominalist about common natures, though he did think that they were mind-dependent in some robust way (Trentman [133], p. 824; Ross [118]). Thus, he rejects Scotus' more-robust realism about common natures. How then is Suárez different from Ockham? Jorge J.E. Gracia characterizes the differences between Ockham and Suárez in his introduction to Suárez's *Metaphysical Disputation V*:

> But then, one may ask, is Suárez's view any different from Ockham's?...The differences between the two are not easily discernible, but nonetheless they are there. Ockham speaks of the individuality of individual composite substances apart from the individuality of their components. But Suárez analyzes the individual of composite substances in terms of the individuality of their components (Gracia [60], p. 21).

Thus, it would seem that Suárez locates the primitive individuation at a lower hylomorphic level than does Ockham. Nevertheless, Suárez does sound like Ockham at times:

> "[I]t must be said that all things that are actual beings or that exist or can exist immediately, are singular and individual" I

say "immediately" in order to exclude the common natures of beings which, as such, cannot immediately exist or have actual entity, except in singular and individual entities (Suárez [130], p. 32).

The question about the difference between Scotus and Suárez on common natures is a difficult one (see Ross [118] for discussion). Suárez thinks that he is far enough from Scotus' moderate realism such that he doesn't face a problem of explaining how Socrates is an individual. For Suárez, Socrates is made of substantial form and matter, and the substantial form (or the substantial form and matter) is self-individuating. Thus he, like Ockham, believes he is able to avoid having to resort to haecceity to individuate Socrates.

In a review of Gracia's translation of Suárez's *Metaphysical Disputation V*, Alfred Freddoso [54] argues that Suárez's position on individuation is an incoherent combination of the views of Scotus and Ockham. Scotus thinks that the common nature *humanity* is made particular by Socrates' haecceity. Ockham eliminates the common nature from the form of Socrates altogether, so there is nothing that needs to be made particular. Suárez seems to agree with Ockham that the common nature is a conceptual entity, yet he also seems to agree with Scotus that it is a constituent of Socrates' substantial form. It is not clear how these two claims are consistent, says Freddoso:

> Suarez's compromise is a mystifying amalgam of these two perfectly intelligible, though contrary, positions. With Ockham, he affirms that *human being* is a conceptual rather than a real entity. Nonetheless, he concurs with Scotus (i) that Socrates can correctly be said to be composed "metaphysically" of *human being* plus something else and (ii) that this something else is real rather than conceptual. He then claims (p. 52 [of Gracia's translation of *Metaphysical Disputation V*]) in the spirit of Ockham that the composition is itself conceptual and not real. So Socrates, a real individual, is composed metaphysically though only conceptually of something real (the individuator) and something conceptual (*human being*)! (Freddoso [54], p. 419).

Freddoso may well be right about Suárez's overall view here. At the very least, it is easy to see that at times, Suárez sounds very much like Ockham and at other times tries to negotiate a position between that of Scotus and Ockham.

There may be a coherent position for Suárez to have staked out, however. In the first of our series of five questions we asked of Scotus (in Section 1.1.1), we noted that for Scotus, *humanity* is in some way common, though not as common as to be a universal. Imagine that it were made even less common; could it be made particular enough to where there was no additional element necessary to contract it into a particular? Or perhaps *humanity* could be fully a particular and in no way common between Socrates and Plato. It could nevertheless be a real constituent of Socrates' (and Plato's) substantial form. In this regard, it would be something more than a merely conceptual entity, as it is for Ockham. We could add to this the claim that Suárez makes about form being the element that individuates Socrates, though without the addition of the haecceity as insisted by Scotus. On this view, then, form could individuate through having as a part the already-particular nature. Or, perhaps more plausibly, form could individuate in a primitive fashion, as suggested in the second question in our series of questions we asked of Scotus (in Section 1.1.1). Either would seem to be a view available to Suárez that makes consistent various different claims about individuation that we find in Suárez. However, I don't think any of these views on which the common nature is a real entity in substantial form are consistent with the other claims that we see in Suárez that echo Ockham's view that natures are merely conceptual entities.

Suárez was read carefully by Leibniz, to whom we turn now.

1.4 G.W. Leibniz

Leibniz was deeply influenced by scholastic metaphysics, particularly by the metaphysics of Scotus and Suárez. Leibniz was perhaps at his most scholastic in his early work (1663) *Disputatio Metaphysica De Principio Individui*. It is also there where he directly addresses haecceity. Here, I want to consider his thoughts on haecceity and individuation from the *Disputatio*.

In the *Disputatio*, Leibniz takes material objects to be composites of substantial form and matter. We also find him there advocating nominalism of an Ockhamist sort about universals and things like Scotus' common nature: [16]

> If there are no universals before the operation of the mind, there is no composition from the universal and the individuating [cause or principle] before the operation of the mind. For there is no real composition, not all of whose members are real. But the first is true. Therefore, etc. (*Disputatio* 23, p. 65).[17,18]

In Leibniz, as in Ockham, thoroughgoing nominalism is crucial to the rejection of haecceity. In particular, if there is no common nature between Socrates and Plato, there is no fear of identifying Socrates and Plato.

How are Socrates and Plato individuated, then? In his position in the *Disputatio*, he echoes Ockham and (in places) Suárez:

"I maintain: every individual is individuated by its whole entity (*Disputatio* 4, p. 100)."[19]

In the *Disputatio* 20 (McCollough [91], pp. 60–61), Leibniz mounts a series of attacks on Scotus' and Scotists' arguments for haecceity.[20] I want to consider here three of these arguments with Leibniz's replies. Leibniz doesn't develop the Scotistic arguments in great depth, and his replies are terse. Nevertheless, we can see Leibniz's Ockhamist sort of reply to Scotus in them.

The first Scotistic argument Leibniz considers proceeds as follows:

> The first argument on Scotus' behalf, which he himself proposed...is as follows. Every unity follows upon some entity. Therefore, numerical [unity follows upon numerical entity]. But that entity is not that which is included in species. Therefore, there is something super-added to species, namely individual difference [haecceity] (McCollough [91], p. 60).

The reasoning attributed to Scotus is something like the following. We get thinghood from some entity. So [pointing at Socrates] he, Socrates, is a thing as the result of some entity. Presumably, this thinghood-conferring entity will be part of substantial form. We already have the common nature as part of substantial form; but it can't bestow thinghood on Socrates, as it is common to Plato. So, we must add ("super-add") something to Socrates' substantial form to make Socrates a thing. That something we add is haecceity.

Leibniz replies that we don't need to add anything to get Socrates to be a thing. He's already a thing:

> I reply that unity follows entity in concept; it is the same in the thing. Neither does numerical entity differ really from specific [entity] (McCollough [91], p. 60).

The second Scotistic argument Leibniz considers is that which he takes to be Scotus' main argument for haecceity. Leibniz's rendering of the argument involves something like the following sort of reasoning. Species (or common nature) for Scotus is shared between individuals of the same kind. The thing that is common must be contracted by some mechanism. Scotus has argued that the other mechanisms for contracting (e.g. double negation and matter) don't work to contract the common nature. Therefore, haecceity must do it:

> Species is not contracted either through form or through matter, or through accidents, etc. Therefore, there remains haecceity (McCollough [91], p. 60).

Leibniz rejects the need for the nature to be contracted, because he denies it is a part of substantial form. There is nothing in terms of nature that Socrates and Plato truly have in common.

> I answer that it is contracted through nothing, because there is no [species] outside the mind (McCollough [91], p. 60).

A third Scotistic argument Leibniz considers centers on the need for some sort of primitive individuation. Individuation must stop at some point with something that is individual in itself. Scotus thinks that the primitive individuation needs to come at the level of haecceity:

> Those things that differ do so through something already diverse. Thus Socrates and Plato [differ] through some ultimate difference, namely haecceity (McCollough [91], p. 60).

In reply, Leibniz locates the primitive individuation in the thing itself, rather than in something like haecceity which is added to the thing:

> I answer: "Those thing that differ ... " must be qualified, by adding: "unless they are themselves already diverse and differ from themselves through something [already diverse]," etc. Hence, I deny the minor (McCollough [91], p. 60).

We are able to see in these arguments and replies Leibniz's Ockhamist style of rejection of Scotus. In particular, we should note two important features of Leibniz's replies. First, self-individuating entities are in no need of anything like haecceity to individuate them. Second, there is no common nature in objects in the world, and thus, there is not any proper concern of having to identify entities (like Socrates and Plato) that would share a common nature.

Just after addressing these arguments from Scotus, Leibniz makes clear that he believes that the formal distinction is crucial to Scotus' account of haecceity. Recall that Scotus claims that the common nature and haecceity are only formally distinct (rather than mentally or really distinct). In *Disputatio* 22, Leibniz says:

> If genus and difference are distinguished only mentally, there is no individual difference [haecceity]. But the first is true. Therefore, etc. The major is plain, for species and numerical difference will also be distinguished only mentally. The minor is proved [as follows]. (1) Those things that differ before the operation of the mind are separable. But genus and differences cannot be separated... (2) Superior differences are predicated of inferiors, e.g., "this rationality is rationality." Therefore, specific difference includes in itself the difference of genus. Therefore, it does not differ from genus (McCollough [91], p. 63).

If the haecceity is only mentally distinct from the common nature, it can't do the work that Scotus wants it to do, says Leibniz (agreeing with Scotus). The arguments that they are mentally distinct that Leibniz provides may beg the question against Scotus, however; they move from the inseparability of haecceity and nature (and thus no real distinction) to the mental distinction of haecceity and nature (with the hidden premise that those are the only two options).

Leibniz focuses his attack on the formal distinction in *Disputatio* 24 and 25 by asking about the grounding of the formal distinction. He seems to think that it must be grounded in the operations of human minds and deduces various problems for this view:

> [Scotists] are exceedingly ambiguous and inconsistent as to when these distinctions are to be applied in actual practice. For, if haecceity differs from species only in that it is apt to move the intellect distinctly [as Leibniz says some Scotists say], how poorly is it brought forward as the principle of individuation, which [principle] ought to be sought apart from the intellect (*Disputatio* 24, McCollough [91], pp. 65–66).

But it's not clear why Scotus wouldn't insist that the formal distinction is a real feature of the world that exists independently of our minds. McCullough (who translated and wrote a commentary on the English version of this work by Leibniz) himself thinks that a core problem with Leibniz's reasoning in this part of the *Disputatio* is that he attributes to Scotus the false (by Scotus' own lights) view that common natures are universals. As we have seen, Scotus, following Avicenna, denies that the common nature is a universal. It's not obvious to me that this (mis)attribution to Scotus is a core element of Leibniz's reasoning in this section of the text. But Leibniz does seem to think that Scotus must accept that the formal distinction is something mind-dependent, and, as such, isn't something that can be a part of grounding individuation in the world. However, there appears to be nothing in Scotus to commit him to the mind-dependence of the formal distinction.

During the early modern period, philosophers moved away from hylomorphic conceptions of metaphysics. (Leibniz was the exception to this, who held onto a background structure of Aristotelian metaphysics even in his mature work.)[21] Roughly, two-hundred years pass before we find another important figure considering the nature and existence of haecceity. That figure is C.S. Peirce.

1.5   C.S. Peirce

In Pierce's own assessment of himself, Peirce was greatly influenced by Scotus:

> The works of Duns Scotus have strongly influenced me. If his logic and metaphysics, not slavishly worshipped, but torn away from its medievalism, be adapted to modern culture, under continual wholesome reminders of nominalistic criticisms, I am convinced that it will go far toward supplying the philosophy which is best to harmonize with physical science (1.6).[22]

Furthermore, Peirce is widely thought to follow Scotus in a belief in haecceity. It's worth taking a look at Peirce's metaphysics to see in what sense he agreed with Scotus about haecceity.[23]

Peirce was influenced by Kant's use of categories in the *Critique of Pure Reason*. Peirce set out to develop his own categories for use in his own metaphysical theorizing. By 1885, he had settled on three terms: Quality, Reaction, and Mediation. He prefers to call each, Firstness, Secondness, and Thirdness, respectively (and we will use these latter three terms for the three categories). Jeffrey R. Di Leo characterizes the three as follows:

> Firstness is the mode of being of that which is such as it is, positively and without reference to anything else. It is considered a possibility, potentiality, or quality and "is perfectly simple and without part; everything has its quality" (1.531).
>
> Secondness is an idea of fact, struggle, or "hereness and nowness." It is the shock of reaction between ego and non-ego, whose very essence is its "thisness."...[T]he term that best characterizes secondness is "fact," viz., secondness comprises the actual facts.
>
> [U]nlike secondness and firstness which are merely experienced and non-cognitive and incapable of being known, thirdness is cognition, viz., it is the mode of being of that which is as such as it is in bringing firstness and secondness into relation with each other (Di Leo [48], pp. 88–89).

In many places, Peirce identifies secondness and haecceity:

> As "pure secondness", haecceity is
>
> "not a conception, nor is it a particular quality. It is an experience. It comes out most fully in the shock of reaction between the ego and non-ego. It is there the double consciousness of effort and resistance. That is something which cannot properly

be conceived. For to conceive it is to generalize it; and to generalize it is to miss altogether the *here*ness and *now*ness which is its essence (8.266) (Di Leo [48], p. 92)."

For Peirce here, haecceity is a sort of experience. Elsewhere, Peirce takes haecceity to be an object of direct reference:

> A sign which denotes a thing by forcing it upon the attention is called an *index*. An index does not describe the qualities of an object. An object, in so far as it is denoted by an index, having *thisness*, and distinguishing itself from other things by its continuous identity and forcefulness, but not by any distinguishing characters, may be called a hecceity [sic] (3.434.)

These two accounts of haecceity are not necessarily inconsistent. It may be that we take the experience, that is, secondness, to be an object and allow it to be denoted directly by an index. (We might then wonder if the experience ceases to be an haecceity when it's not picked out with a demonstrative.) It's not clear to me if Peirce would accept this squaring of his different accounts of haecceity.

It is also not clear to me, in spite of his various attempts at explanation, precisely what haecceity *is* for Peirce. Peirce's writing is turgid, even by the standards of the 19th century. It does seem clear that whatever haecceity is for Peirce, it doesn't correspond to Scotus' use of the term. Robert Almeder states this view:

> Nor does *Haecceitas*, as Scotus conceived it, correspond with the category of Secondness with Peirce often equated with the Scotistic principle of individuation. No doubt, Peirce used Secondness as a principle of individuation just as Scotus used *Haecceitas* as a principle of individuation, but in Peirce it is not altogether clear precisely what is the ontological status of that which Secondness is supposed to individuate (Almeder [9], p. 14).

Scotus thinks that the haecceity is a hylomorphically simple entity that renders the common nature and thus the substantial form particular. Whatever it is for Peirce, it is not that. In the next section when we begin considering figures from the 20th century, we will see that haecceity becomes a sort of property. It doesn't seem to be that for Peirce, either.

Thus, it's not clear to me that we find in Peirce a notion of haecceity worth developing further. In this, he differs from Scotus, and in the 20th century, he differs from people like Roderick Chisholm, Robert Adams and Alvin Plantinga.

We turn to the development of haecceity in the 20th century now. It is during this time that haecceity becomes a property that is instantiated across possible worlds by one and only one object. There are four principal figures who develop a metaphysics of haecceity in the 20th century: Alvin Plantinga, Roderick Chisholm, Robert Adams, and Gary Rosenkrantz. We will consider each of these figures, beginning with Alvin Plantinga.

1.6   Alvin Plantinga

Alvin Plantinga first speaks of haecceities in his paper "World and Essence" from 1970. Plantinga there (and elsewhere) takes haecceities to be properties, rather than constituents of a substantial form in the way Scotus thinks of them. (Indeed, Plantinga's metaphysics are not hylomorphic in any sense.) In "World and Essence," he identifies essences, haecceities, and individual concepts. There, an haecceity/essence/individual concept is a property F of an object x that is such that: (i) necessarily if x exists, x has F; and (ii) necessarily, nothing distinct from x has F (Plantinga [110], p. 70).[24]

Four years later in *The Nature of Necessity*, the above definition is now a characterization of *essence*. In this later work, there are two sorts of essences. One is a particular sort of *world-indexed property*. Let 'α' be a name of the actual world. Consider some object x and some property F that x has in the actual world. The property *having F in α* then will be *essential to x*. That is, it will be the case that: necessarily, if x exists, x has the property *having F in α*. Suppose, though, that x is the only entity who actually exemplifies F. Then, *having F in α* will be an *essence* of x: x will be such that necessarily if x exists, x exemplifies *having F in α*, and necessarily, nothing distinct from x exemplifies *having F in α*.

So, some world-indexed properties are essences for Plantinga. The other sort of essence is an haecceity. An haecceity is a primitive identity property, expressed by a gerundial phrase of the form "being identical with N" or "being N" where "N" is some rigid term (like a name or indexical). Thus, *being identical with Socrates* is an haecceity, as is *being that book*. For Plantinga, haecceities exist necessarily and are not dependent on the objects that instantiate them (Plantinga [107, 109]). They are wholly abstract entities and aren't structured by way of having concrete individuals as constituents or parts of them. They also aren't in any sense parts of things that instantiate them.

Plantinga makes considerable use of haecceities in his metaphysics and philosophy of language. In *The Nature of Necessity*, he takes them to be the semantic contents of proper names. This allows empty names to retain semantic contents, as many think they don't if individuals are semantic contents of names. (Later, Plantinga takes names to express world-indexed essences (Plantinga [106]).) He also uses necessarily existing haecceities to stand in for merely possible, nonactual individuals in his modal metaphysics. This allows him to give a metaphysics inspired by the Kripke semantics for modal logic that employs only existing entities (Plantinga [105]). (We will consider this use of haecceities further in Chapter 5.)

1.7 Roderick Chisholm

Although Chisholm mentions haecceities as far back as 1963 in his review of Jaakko Hintikka's *Knowledge and Belief* [27], it is in *Person and Object* from 1976 where Chisholm first carefully investigates haecceity. His definition of haecceity in *Person and Object* is equivalent to Plantinga's definition of essence in *The Nature of Necessity*:

> D.I.5 G is an *individual essence* (or *haecceity*) =Df G is a property which is such that, for every x, x has G if and only if it is necessarily such that it has G, and it is impossible that there is a y other than x such that y has G (Chisholm [25], p. 29).[25]

According to Chisholm, when I use the word "I," I am directly aware of myself and grasp my own haecceity (Chisholm [25], pp. 29–35). Furthermore, Chisholm's haecceity is the semantic content of "I" when he uses it:

> The foregoing [reasoning from *Person and Object*, ch. 1], then, suggests a general interpretation of the first-person pronoun: The first-person pronoun is such that, in each person's use of it, it has that person himself as its *reference* and it has his individual essence as its *sense* (Chisholm [31], p. 321).

Chisholm thinks that though I may grasp my own haecceity, I am not able to grasp the haecceity of individuals distinct from me:

> Each person who uses the first person pronoun uses it to refer to himself and in such a way that, in that use, its *Bedeutung* or reference is itself and its *Sinn* or intention is his own individual essence. A corollary would be that, whereas each person knows directly and immediately certain propositions implying his own individual essence, no one knows any propositions implying the individual essence of anyone else (Chisholm [25], p. 36).

In 1979 in a reply to a collection of essays on his work, we find that Chisholm has changed his mind about haecceities (Chisholm [31]). He no longer thinks they exist. There he says that the propositions I grasp about myself are purely qualitative. Indeed, Chisholm in 1979 is inclined to the view that all properties are qualitative.

> Plantinga [in an essay on Chisholm's metaphysics (Plantinga [102])] suggests a distinction between what he calls "qualitative" properties and "quidditative" properties...I think that the distinction is an important one. I would express my present view as one which is sceptical with respect to quidditative properties. I suggest, then, that we consider the possibility that all properties are qualitative (Chisholm [31], p. 323).

Chisholm most thoroughly develops his metaphysics without haecceities in his 1986 paper, "Possibility without Haecceity." There he says that the nonexistence of haecceities has significant consequences for our understanding of what it is to exist in a possible world. In particular, we are not able to give a Plantinga-style [101] gloss on claims of the form "x exists in W" (for Plantinga: x exists in W just if necessarily, if W is actual, x exists):

> If there are no haecceities, then for any world W, I might not have existed in W. "If I have no individual essence, then we cannot say of any world that it is necessarily such that I exist...Indeed if neither you or I have individual essences, then the prevailing world could have obtained with you playing my role and me playing yours...We cannot say, therefore, that "x exists in W" means the same as "If W were to obtain, then x would exist." For I exist in this world, but this world could have obtained without me (Chisholm [26], p. 46).

There is an assumption in Chisholm here that transworld identity requires haecceity. This, I think, is not the case. Transworld identity could be brute (see Chapter 3 for more on this). But if Chisholm is right, his denial of haecceity makes it impossible to give actualist truth conditions for basic modal metaphysical claims.

In "Possibility without Haecceity," Chisholm questions his past reasoning that expressions like "I" and "being identical with Socrates" have haecceities as semantic contents. He wonders why we should think that expressions like "I" and "Socrates" have semantic contents at all:

> But why assume that terms such as "Socrates" and "I" *have* senses? One can describe their use adequately without such an assumption. The function of proper names in a language may be described without presupposing that they have senses. The same applies to pronouns and demonstratives (Chisholm [26], p. 47).

As we will see in the next section, Robert Adams thinks that haecceities are contingent existents that are dependent on the individuals that instantiate them. Chisholm, on the contrary, believes that if there were haecceities, they would exist necessarily (Chisholm [26], p. 44). More generally, he maintains abstracta aren't dependent on contingent things for their existence (Chisholm [26], p. 46). (It is not clear what Chisholm would say about sets with contingent members.)

1.8 Robert Adams

In three important papers in the late 1970s and 1980s, Robert Adams develops a theory of haecceities (Adams [4, 5, 6]).[26,27] Adams' work on haecceities is perhaps the most influential such work in modern times. In his 1979 "Primitive Thisness and Primitive Identity," Adams argues that haecceities (which he calls "thisnesses") are necessary for individuating material objects. Like Plantinga, Adams thinks haecceities are primitive properties that don't have constituents and aren't parts of things that instantiate them. However, unlike Plantinga, he thinks that haecceities depend for their existence on the things that instantiate them. In "Primitive Thisness and Primitive Identity," Adams gives a series of arguments that are designed to show that there are some possible cases of numerical diversity the grounding of which require haecceities. (We will consider these arguments in depth in Chapter 3.) Adams' best-known arguments for haecceity employ Max Black's famous example of two qualitatively identical iron spheres (Black [18]). Black thinks that invoking haecceities to individuate the spheres is a sort of cheat, as there is something trivial about identity properties. (We will discuss this in Section 3.2.1.) Adams disagrees. He argues that individuating the spheres at different places and at different times requires haecceities. We also need haecceities to distinguish between worlds where there are one and two spheres.

In his 1981 paper "Actualism and Thisness," Adams considers the consequences of the thesis that haecceities depend for their existence on the things that instantiate them. (We will explore this issue in detail in Chapter 5.) Adams agrees with Plantinga that *actualism* is true. Actualism is, as Plantinga puts it, the view that necessarily there are no nonexistent objects.[28] As we noted earlier, Plantinga uses haecceities to stand in for nonexistent objects in his modal metaphysics. Adams isn't able to do this, as he argues there are no haecceities of nonexistent objects. As a result, Adams devotes a great deal of space in the paper to explaining how propositions like *it is possible that Socrates not exist* could be true.

In his 1986 paper "Time and Thisness," Adams argues that there are no future entities. As a result, there are no haecceities of future individuals.

24 Preliminaries

But haecceities of past individuals are available to us to grasp and consider, and thus exist.

In Chapters 3 and 5, we will closely look at Adams' reasoning around the existence and nature of haecceities.

1.9   Gary Rosenkrantz

In 1993, Gary Rosenkrantz published *Haecceity: An Ontological Essay*. Prior to this book (the one that you are reading), Rosenkrantz's book was the only book-length treatment focused entirely on haecceity.

Rosenkrantz's conception of haecceity echoes that of Plantinga's. For Rosenkrantz, an haecceity is a abstract identity property:

> The time has come for a summary of the implications of my arguments... Firstly, there are nonqualitative haecceities. Secondly, a nonqualitative haecceity is a property, a kind of *abstractum*. Thirdly, a nonqualitative haecceity cannot be identified with an *abstractum* of another category such as a relation, a proposition, or a set (Rosenkrantz [117], p. 139).

Haecceities are primitive; they don't have individuals as constituents (Rosenkrantz [117], pp. 114 ff.). Furthermore, necessarily, every object has an haecceity, and there are haecceities for concrete objects that don't exist (Rosenkrantz [117], pp. 140 ff.)

For Rosenkrantz, most haecceities cannot be grasped, even by God.

> Although I have argued that none of us ever grasps the haecceity of a physical object or person other than himself, I have yet to argue [this is] an *impossibility*. Edward Wierenga is a philosopher who believes it is possible for someone to grasp the haecceity of a person other than himself...he maintains there is no reason to deny that *God* grasps the haecceity of persons other than himself. I will argue that Wierenga's position is untenable, and that a person grasping the haecceity of a physical object or person other than himself is an impossibility (Rosenkrantz [117], p. 220).

We will consider in Chapter 6 his argument against our being able to grasp most haecceities.

According to Rosenkrantz, I am able to grasp only my own haecceity, as well as that of some of my mental states and those of some abstracta:

> In his early writings Russell was inclined to believe that a person is acquainted with himself, his own sense-data, and certain

abstract entities...I argue that it is plausible that each of us is acquainted (in my sense) [which involves grasping an haecceity] with himself, some of his own mental states, and a variety of abstract entities (Rosenkrantz [117], p. 225).

Rosenkrantz's principal argument for haecceities is that they are required to individuate material objects. He argues for this claim by considering what he takes to be all other possible individuators for material objects and arguing that none are sufficient for individuating material objects (Rosenkrantz [117], ch. 2). (We will consider this argument further in Chapter 3.) Abstract objects, however, are not individuated by haecceities. Rather, their distinctness is primitive (Rosenkrantz [117], p. 137). So, haecceities aren't themselves individuated by haecceities, though they do have them (Rosenkrantz [117], p. 132).

1.10 Conclusion

In this first chapter, we have considered different conceptions of haecceity, from Scotus in the late 13th and early 14th centuries to Gary Rosenkrantz in the late 20th century. We have seen how haecceity begins as a part of substantial form in Scotus, and this is the notion of haecceity that Ockham, Suárez, and Leibniz attack. When haecceity is revived in the 20th century in the work of people like Adams, Chisholm, and Plantinga, it is revived as a property that individuates. To the present day, haecceity usually is taken to be some sort of property.

In the next chapter, we will consider carefully different positions one might take as to the nature of haecceity. The positions that we set out and investigate in the second chapter will be informed by the various views we have encountered in this first chapter.

Notes

1 Most scholars think that Scotus first used the Latin "haecceitas" or "haecitas," although there is no unanimity on this issue. See Andrews [10] for discussion.
2 References to Scotus' *Ordinatio* are from Spade [126].
3 Bates [13] claims that the latter is Scotus' main concern. We cover the distinction further in Section 3.1.1.
4 Then, for Scotus, the haecceity, as part of substantial form, isn't anything like a property.
5 Real distinctness entails distinctness in the contemporary sense, though the converse entailment doesn't hold.
6 So far as I can tell, there is no consensus among Scotus scholars as to the precise nature of the formal distinction. This is in spite of the fact that there has been a great deal written on the topic (see, e.g. Gelber [58], Jordan [74], Grajewski [61], Adams [1], Bates [13], Henry [65], King [78]). King [78] and others seem

to think that if x and y are formally distinct, then x=y. Formally distinct x and y differ only in (to borrow a contemporary locution) modes of presentation. Others seem to think that if x and y are formally distinct, then x≠y; though x and y are closely connected in some sort of way.

7 Most commentators on Scotus think that the formal distinction of haecceity and common nature is an important part of Scotus' metaphysics of individuation. Some (e.g. King [78], p. 60) think that it isn't important for Scotus. It is not clear to me why Scotus needs the haecceity and nature to be formally distinct. Part of this is that it's not clear to me what the formal distinction amounts to, especially as it relates to our post-Frege contemporary notions of identity and distinctness (see note 6). Perhaps Scotus needs some sort of way of distinguishing things such that he can say there are two things, but they aren't separable (recall that the medieval "real distinction" involves not just distinctness in our contemporary sense, but separability). This seems plausible–there is conceptual room for a distinction of this sort–until one realizes that divine attributes distinct in this way would seem to violate divine simplicity. The formal distinction is accepted by most medievals—Ockham included—as applying to the divine attributes of a simple God.

8 See Wolter [142] for further discussion of the arguments.

9 Thus, a nominalist like Ockham will have to account in some other way for our knowledge that distinct individuals may be of the same type. Another, related problem for Ockham is that without real common natures in the world, something like conventionalism might seem to have to be true. (Compare to the problems Locke is thought to have if there isn't any fundamental difference between nominal and real essence.) For analysis of both of these problems for Ockham, I refer the reader to Marilyn Adams' excellent discussion in Adams [2], ch. 4.

10 This question is generated, in part, from my inability to understand how anything other than a truly particular nature isn't thereby universal.

11 Page numbers from Ockham's *Ordinatio* are to Spade [126].

12 I elided some of Ockham's discussion here, which includes a fair amount of direct or almost-direct quotation from Scotus. The quotation is also elided in Spade's translation [126], pp. 153–154.

13 See, e.g. Ord. d. 2, qq. 4–7 (reprinted in Spade [126], pp. 114–190); his *Commentary on Abelard's Sentences* I, DII, Q4 (reprinted in Hyman and Walsh [68] pp 662. ff.); his *Summa Logicae* I, c. xv (reprinted in Boehner [97] pp. 35 ff.)

14 See Adams [2] ch. 2 for a very clear discussion.

15 For discussion, see Adams [2], pp. 43ff. and Maurer [90], pp. 74 ff.

16 I should note that Suárez usually is taken to be the primary scholastic influence on Leibniz (e.g. see McCullough [91] and Cover/O'Leary-Hawthorne [33]). While Leibniz read Scotus and his followers through the lens of Suárez and Scotists like Fonseca, Pererius, and Bassolis; Leibniz's own views appear to most closely mirror those of Ockham. However, Ockham's own writings don't appear to have been carefully studied by Leibniz (Martin [89], p. 182).

17 Leibniz also was a nominalist in his later work. See e.g Leibniz ([80] section 47; [79], section 323).

18 All references (including page numbers) to Leibniz's *Disputatio* are from McCullough's translation in McCullough [91].
19 There is reason to think that Leibniz shifts his position on individuation in his later work. In places like the *Discourse* we see Leibniz arguing that each substance is individuated by the qualities it has. Indeed, for later Leibniz it is impossible that two objects have all the same qualities.
20 There is some reason to doubt the accuracy of Leibniz's rendering of Scotus' or Scotists' arguments. See McCullough [91] ch. 3 for discussion. My main concern here is examining Leibniz's reasoning around haecceity, and will eschew questions of the fidelity of Leibniz's interpretations.
21 Leibniz's later work certainly *sounds* less scholastic and Aristotelian than his earlier work, and we find several places where Leibniz claims to have rejected hylomorphic metaphysics in his adoption of the new mechanistic philosophy. But to the end he thought in Aristotelian terms and remained much more scholastic than his peers. See Garber [57] for discussion.
22 All quotations from Peirce are from Peirce's Collected Works [100].
23 There has been a great deal written about Peirce and Scotus. In what follows, I draw primarily from Di Leo [48], Almeder [9], and Boler [19]. Jeffery Di Leo's "Peirce's Haecceitism" [48] was particularly helpful to me.
24 All page references to Plantinga's essays are to the collection of essays (Plantinga [108]).
25 Chisholm uses "individual essence" and "haecceity" interchangeably. He first does this in his 1975 paper, "Individuation: Some Thomistic Questions and Answers," (Chisholm [28], p. 29); and later in "Objects and Persons: Revisions and Replies" (Chisholm [31], pp. 319 ff.), and "Possibility without Haecceity" (Chisholm [26], p. 45).
26 Adams talks about haecceities in two other later places. These are: in his recent book *What Is and What Is in Itself* (Adams [8]), and in his 1997 paper "Thisness and Time Travel" (Adams [7]). In each he adopts his earlier theorizing about haecceities without adding to it.
27 Adams credits interactions with David Kaplan as leading to his work on haecceity in the 1970s. He says that "In conversations I had with David Kaplan...we began to speak of belief in irreducible thisness as "Haecceitism" (Adams [8], p. 133). In his published work, Kaplan himself doesn't discuss at any length haecceities. He does discuss "haecceitism," though his conception of the term is different than that of Adams. For Kaplan [75] haecceitism is the view that there is transworld identity. This was a controversial notion in 1975 when Kaplan published his thoughts on haecceitism. Many philosophers were under the sway of Quine who thought that it didn't make sense to think of identity across possible worlds; in part because reference was always under a description, and thus we had no way to identify an object from world to world.
28 Adams conception is slightly different than this; see Davidson [47], ch. 1 for discussion.

2 The Nature of Haecceity

In the first chapter, we looked at different conceptions of haecceity through history. In this chapter, we will try to get clearer about what haecceity is—about what kind of thing plays the haecceity functional role.[1] In the first section of the chapter, I will state three distinct views of haecceity, namely, *partism*, *primitivism*, and *constituentism*. We will consider the subspecies of the first and third of these types of views. I am particularly concerned in this chapter with getting clear on the logical space of potential views of haecceity; so, we will encounter several views that don't (so far as I know) have adherents. (But perhaps in some cases they should!) In the second section of the chapter, I will defend one of these options, *sui generis* constituentism.

2.1 Three Types of Haecceity: Some Statements

We begin by stating three different conceptions of haecceity. We have seen defenders of the first two views, partism and primitivism, in Chapter 1.

2.1.1 Partism

The first major subdivision in our classification of views about haecceity is *partism*. According to the partist about haecceity, an haecceity is a part, in some robust sense of "part," of objects that exemplify or have it. There are two varieties of partism about haecceity, *hylomorphic partism* and *non-hylomorphic partism*. The hylomorphic partist adopts an Aristotelian ontology of form and matter and thinks that haecceities are parts of objects within this framework. As we saw in the last chapter, Scotus is a hylomorphic partist. He thinks that haecceities are parts of substantial forms. They contract the common nature, which is also part of substantial form. The common nature is made particular by the haecceity, and this yields individual material objects. As a result, Socrates is an individual and is distinct from Plato in spite of the fact that they share a common nature, *humanity*. They are individuals and distinct from each other, because each

A Taxonomy of Partism

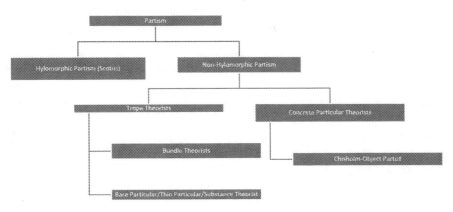

Figure 2.1 A taxonomy of partism

has their own haecceity that makes individual the common nature *humanity* in each.

There are presumably other sorts of hylomorphic partism that one might adopt. These would have the haecceity interacting differently with the form-matter composite so as to individuate the object in question. For instance, rather than individuating part of substantial form *a la* Scotus, perhaps haecceity could individuate matter directly. This would be a hylomorphic partism that was closer to a view of individuation like that of Aristotle or (at times) Aquinas. I am not aware of anyone who defends a hylomorphic partism about haecceity that is different than that of Scotus. But *a priori*, there is at least one other hylomorphic partism distinct from Scotus'.

The non-hylomorphic partist believes that haecceities are parts of objects, though objects themselves are not composites of form and matter. There is a further distinction among non-hylomorphic partists, between those that think that an haecceity is a trope and those who think it's a concrete particular. One sort of trope non-hylomorphic partist is a bundle theorist about objects. They take the haecceity to be one trope among many, the bundle of which is a material object. Another sort of trope non-hylomorphic partist believes in substance/thin particulars/bare particulars. They take the haecceity to be one trope among many that inheres in the substance/thin particular/bare particular.

At one point in his career, Roderick Chisholm proposed the view that we are identical with simple, point-sized objects that are located within a human body. Call these (following Peter van Inwagen [137]) "Chisholm objects." There is a potential concrete particular non-hylomorphic partist view that bears some similarity to Chisholm's view about the nature of the person. On this view, the haecceity is a concrete particular that is something like a Chisholm object. Rather than being identical with a Chisholm object, each material object has as a part an haecceity that is simple and point-sized. Call this view "Chisholm-object partism." Chisholm-object partism is a variety of non-hylomorphic partism on which haecceities are concrete particulars.

2.1.2 Primitivism

The second major subdivision in our classification of views about haecceity is *primitivism*. The primitivist about haecceity thinks that haecceities are primitive properties that don't have individuals as constituents. For the primitivist, the property *being Socrates* is a primitive entity that lacks constituents and thus lacks Socrates as a constituent. This is a most widely held view among contemporary defenders of haecceity. Primitivism counts among its proponents Alvin Plantinga, Robert Adams, Gary Rosenkrantz, David Ingram [71], and Joseph Diekemper [50]. We see a particularly clear statement and endorsement of primitivism from Ingram:

> [T]hisnesses are primitive properties. As such, thisnesses cannot be reduced to (or analysed in terms of) any purely qualitative properties or relations to other objects. *Qua* primitive properties, thisnesses are to be understood as simple, unstructured entities. Thisnesses are properties, but they comprise a *sui generis* category of properties (Ingram [70], p. 443).[2]

2.1.3 Constituentism

The third major subdivision in our classification of views about haecceity is *constituentism*. The constituentist about haecceities thinks that haecceities have individuals that exemplify them as constituents. Thus, the property *being Socrates* has, as a constituent, Socrates. I don't know of anyone who defends constituentism, though Nathan Salmon mentions (seemingly favorably) haecceities having constituents in a footnote in *Reference and Essence* (Salmon [119], p. 21). There are at least two different sorts of constituentism. On the first, *slot-theoretic constituentism*, an haecceity is the the result of "plugging" an individual into the *is identical with* relation. Gary Rosenkrantz states (though he himself rejects) this view:

> (C1d) The haecceity of a particular, *a*, is the property of being identical with *a*, and this property has *a* and the relation of Identity as logical constituents.
>
> [T]he compound relational property of being identical with *a* derives from *a*'s being "plugged" into the right hand variable

position in the relation _being identical with_, resulting in the monadic attribute _being identical with *a* (Rosenkrantz [117], p. 114).

On this view, the relation *is identical with* contains gaps or *slots*, as Cody Gilmore [59] calls them. The theorist who thinks that the *is identical with* relation has slots presumably thinks that relations and properties in general have slots in them. Thus, the slot-theoretic constituentist presumably then is a *slot theorist* in Gilmore's terminology. Gilmore characterizes the view as follows:

> Slot theory, as I use the term, is the view that (i) there exist such entities as argument places, or 'slots', in universals, and that (ii) a universal u is n-adic if and only if there are n slots in u (Gilmore [59], p. 187).

Kit Fine [53] has argued that slot theoretic views (which he calls *positionalist* views) of relations suffer from ontological profligacy in that they posit too many entities in the world that explain the holding of relations. Fine calls these "completions." I am unpersuaded by Fine's arguments that there is an implausible multiplication of completions on a slot-theoretic conception of relations. But some metaphysicians find Fine's arguments compelling (e.g. Dixon [51]).

For those who *do* find Fine (or other objections to slot theory) persuasive, there is a second variety of constituentism that one might adopt. On this other constituentist view, the haecceity has an individual as a constituent and the "rest" of the haecceity is a *sui generis* abstract entity, *being identical with x*. This *sui generis* abstract entity in a most general sense is a function from objects to haecceities. Call this second view "*sui generis* constituentism." We will consider in greater detail the difference between slot-theoretic and *sui generis* constituentism in the last section of this chapter.

We have before us then three different sorts of views about the nature of haecceity: partism, primitivism, and constituentism. We have subdivisions of partism and constituentism. How should we evaluate these different views? We turn to this question in the next section.

2.2 An Assessment of the Different Views of Haecceity

In the last section, we set out a number of different options for views as to the nature of haecceity. In this section, we assess the different views. What should we make of these different conceptions of haecceity? As I indicated at the start of the chapter, I myself opt for *sui generis* constituentism. Thus, the remainder of this chapter will be, generally speaking, a defense of *sui generis* constituentism. The defense will come in several stages. I will start by rejecting partism. Next, I will argue that constituentism has many explanatory virtues that primitivism lacks. After that, I will consider and reply to a series of objections to constituentism. Finally, I will set out why I favor *sui generis* over slot-theoretic constituentism.

2.2.1 Against Partism

My principal reason for rejecting non-Chisholm-object partism is that I don't believe that objects have haecceities as parts in the way non-Chisholm-object partists believe. This stems from a belief that objects don't have things like tropes or substantial forms as parts. I don't think there is any reason to include such things in one's ontology; there is nothing that substantial forms or tropes do for one metaphysically that one can't already do with objects, properties, and abstract states of affairs.[3] Furthermore, objects, properties, and states of affairs—for me at least—are less metaphysically suspect than abstract particular tropes or form-matter ontologies. Thus, I reject that objects have things like tropes or forms as parts.

If I am asked to name the parts that Socrates has, I might give various sorts of answers, depending on the sort of thing I think Socrates is. For instance, if I think that Socrates is an animal of some sort, I might say that the parts of Socrates include his arms and legs, molecules that make up the arms and legs, atoms that make up the molecules, and quarks and electrons that make up the atoms. If I think that Socrates is a brain, I might say that the parts of Socrates include his hippocampus and amygdala, molecules that compose them, atoms that compose these molecules, and quarks and electrons that compose the atoms. If I think that Socrates is an immaterial mind, I might be inclined to deny that Socrates himself has parts, though his body has as parts molecules, atoms, and subatomic particles.[4] At no point in my list of parts of Socrates have I included things like tropes or substantial forms.

I will say a bit more about why I reject substance (including bare particulars and thin particulars), tropes, and hylomorphic conceptions of metaphysics. Dealing in any thorough manner with any one of these topics would involve a separate book, but I will try to give the reader a sense of why I reject each. Let's begin with substance. We get our contemporary notion of substance as something like a bare or thin particular from Locke's *Essay* (Book 2, Chapter xxiii). Locke conceives of objects as involving collections of qualities. These collections of qualities must include something in which the qualities "inhere"—something that "stands under" or underlies the qualities. This something Locke calls *substance*. The argument that something is required to underlie things like properties or universals has been picked up and defended in more recent times by Bergmann [14] and Armstrong [11], among others. Most objections to something like Lockean substance are leveled at the properties or qualities that the substance is supposed to (or not to) have (see Berkeley [16], Bailey [12], Davidson [45]). These sorts of objections seem to me to have merit.

However, there is another, and in some respects more fundamental, problem with anything like Lockean substance. Philosophers find themselves positing things like Lockean substance as a way to explain collections of properties or universals in the world. We might think of these properties as something like a group of pins. Pins can't stand on their own; they need a pincushion, and substance is that pincushion. However, it seems to me that the world simply *doesn't* have collections of properties or universals in it. Consider my desk. These substance theorists might say that where my desk is located is a collection of properties (or property-like entities) like *being a desk, being made of wood, being brown,* and so on. But it seems to me that in the region of space where my desk is located, there simply aren't collections of these properties. Located in that space is rather the desk and parts of the desk that themselves exemplify properties. Thus, we may say the entire desk exemplifies *being a desk* and *being wooden*. The left half of desk exemplifies the property *being brown* and so on. There aren't any *properties* in the desk-shaped region of space, however. There, rather, is just the desk and parts of it. There is no reason to imagine there being properties collected together in regions of space, particularly once we acknowledge that there are objects that exemplify properties and fill the regions of space. The properties themselves are not spatial or spatially located entities.

I have a similar concern with tropes. Let us set aside standard objections to tropes that center on confusions as to their very nature (e.g. Daly [36]), though I think these objections are powerful. I just don't think there *are* any tropes. The trope theorist would point to my desk and assert that there I may find a trope of brownness. But I don't think there is such an entity there. There is a brown surface.[5] There is a thing—the table, or the table's surface, or both—that exemplifies *being brown*. But there is no *further thing* there that is a trope. We have no need of such entities once we acknowledge the existence of things in the world that exemplify properties.

There are two reasons why I reject form-matter ontologies. The first is that I never feel like I have a firm grasp on what forms, or forms over and above matter, are. So far as I can tell, there is no unified account of the nature of form in Aristotle, and I've not encountered anyone post-Aristotle working in hylomorphic metaphysics who have been able help me to a robust understanding of the fundamentals of that metaphysic.

A second reason is related to the first: I don't think that form-matter ontologies do any explanatory work that ordinary object-property ontologies can't do. This is to say that I think that there is nothing that the

Aristotle of the *Metaphysics* gains over the Aristotle of the *Categories* in terms of explanatory ability. There is a reason why form-matter ontologies were largely abandoned with the development of philosophy and science in the 17th century. We found that we had no need of substantial forms in our physics post Galileo, Kepler, Descartes, and Newton. We also found that we had no need of substantial forms in our philosophy post Descartes and Locke. Philosophers, by and large, found that they could better understand and tackle problems in metaphysics and epistemology without invoking substantial forms. I think that they were right.

Peter van Inwagen argues that ontologies that include things like Lockean substance and tropes (which he dubs "constituent ontologies") are fundamentally incoherent.

> My principal reason for repudiating the idea of ontological structure [that objects have quasi-mereological parts] is...I do not understand the words and phrases that are the typical items of the core vocabulary of any given constituent ontology. "Immanent universal," "trope," "exist wholly in," "wholly present wherever it is instantiated," "constituent of" (said of a universal and a particular in that order): these are mysteries to me (van Inwagen [138], p. 208).

I don't know if I would go so far as van Inwagen does here in claiming that none of these views make sense. For instance, I think I understand, e.g., the non-hylomorphic partist views on which haecceities are quasi-mereological parts of objects. But I just don't think that reality includes substantial forms, tropes, and non-ordinary concrete particulars (bare or thin). Thus, I reject hylomorphic partism, as well as most forms of non-hylomorphic partism.

There is one sort of partism that we haven't considered, however. What of Chisholm-object partism, our representative variety of non-hylomorphic partism on which haecceities are concrete particulars? The Chisholm-object partist thinks that my haecceity is a point-sized simple object that is located somewhere inside me. I have several concerns with Chisholm-object partism. The first objection I have to it centers on its inability to generalize to abstract objects. Maybe abstracta don't have haecceities, but our concept of haecceity shouldn't *a priori* rule out that they could. It is very difficult to see how we construe haecceities of abstract objects on a Chisholm-object partist model. Primitivism and constituentism, by contrast, each allow that abstracta may have haecceities.

Second, if one is concerned about necessary connections between distinct existences, one will be disinclined toward Chisholm-object partism.[6] According to the Chisholm-object partist, it's a necessary truth that my existing entails that my haecceity exists. The original position about the self that Chisholm himself adopted identifies me with a Chisholm object.

Thus, it's trivially true that I exist just if that Chisholm object exists. But the Chisholm-object partist thinks that there is a necessary existential connection between me and my haecceity. This will be unpalatable if one is enticed by Hume's Dictum and similar principles.

Even if one is sanguine about some necessary connections between distinct existences, I still have concerns about the connection between my haecceity and me. Is it a necessary truth that if I'm killed my haecceity ceases to exist? What if my haecceity isn't located in a body: Suppose it is dislodged from my body and is washed down the drain. Do I then exist in the drain because my haecceity exists there? Or do I continue existing where I was before because it is enough that my haecceity exist somewhere? Suppose God destroyed my haecceity while keeping everything else about me the same. Is it metaphysically impossible for me to exist under such circumstances? Would God, in destroying my haecceity, thereby create a duplicate of me?

I think, then, that there are compelling reasons to reject Chisholm-object partism. I also think that there are compelling reasons to reject non-Chisholm-object partism. Thus, I think that we ought not be partists about haecceity. What of constituentism and primitivism? We turn to those views now.

2.2.2 Constituentism vs. Primitivism

2.2.2.1 Advantages of Constituentism

In the last section, I have set out why partism is not an option for me when it comes to elucidating the nature of haecceity. In this section, we will consider the merits of the other two types of theories about haecceity: constituentism and primitivism. According to the constituentist, the haecceity *being Socrates* has the man Socrates as a constituent. According to the primitivist (by far the most-widely-held view about the nature of haecceity), an haecceity has no parts; rather, it is a primitive property. In this section, I want to argue that there are a number of reasons to prefer constituentism to primitivism. In Section 2.2.3, I will argue that though there are several reasons to prefer any constituentism over primitivism, there are reasons to prefer *sui generis* constituentism to both primitivism and slot-theoretic constituentism.

One reason to prefer constituentism to primitivism is that constituentism suggests an account of why haecceities aren't qualitative properties and of the qualitative-quidditative distinction more generally. Often, people handwave at the difference between qualitative and quidditative properties. For instance, primitivist Alvin Plantinga says in "On Existentialism":

> Let us say that a property is *quidditative* if it is either a thisness [haecceity] or involves a thisness in a certain way. We could try to spell out the way in question in formal and recursive details; but instead let me just give some examples. *Being identical with* Nero or *being Nero* is a quidditative property; but so are *being more blood-thirsty than Nero, being either Nero or Cicero, being either Nero or wise, being possibly wiser than Nero, being believed by Nero to be treacherous*, and *being such that there is someone more bloodthirsty than Nero*. We may contrast the notion of a quidditative property with that of a *qualitative* property. Again, I shall not try to give a *definition* of this notion; but examples would be *being wise, being 14 years old, being angry, being learned, being six feet from a desk*, and the like (Plantinga [109], p. 158).

Others have argued that there is no reductive analysis of the qualitative/non-qualitative distinction to be had (Cowling [34]).

The constituentist may say that the difference between a quidditative property like *being Socrates* and a qualitative property like *being wise* is that the former has a concrete individual, Socrates, as a constituent. The haecceity is directly about a concrete individual in a way *being wise* isn't. This sorting of properties into quidditative and qualitative mirrors the distinction between singular and qualitative propositions, where singular propositions about concrete individuals have an individual as a constituent. In Chapter 4, we will explore the qualitative/quidditative distinction, and we will consider how having individuals as constituents of properties may help in distinguishing between qualitative and quidditative properties.

A second reason to prefer constituentism to primitivism is that it allows a uniform semantic treatment of rigid terms. Suppose we think that direct reference is true—that the semantic content of a rigid term like a proper name is the referent of the name. If we are constituentists, we are able to treat "Socrates" in "Socrates is a philosopher" and "Socrates" in "being Socrates" in a semantically equivalent manner. Each introduces the man Socrates into the semantic contents of the linguistic item in question (a proposition and an haecceity, respectively). Either the primitivist needs to deny that "Socrates" is ever directly referential, or she needs to say that "Socrates" varies its semantics between "Socrates is a philosopher" and "being Socrates." I don't think this is a *significant* problem for the primitivist; she may simply insist that "Socrates" isn't a referring term in the context of a gerundial phrase like "being Socrates." But it is a *prima facie* strength of constituentism that the constituentist can give a uniform treatment of the semantics of rigid terms in different contexts.

A third reason to prefer constituentism to primitivism is that constituentism allows us to give an account of the similarity between two haecceities like *being Socrates* and *being Plato*. The slot-theoretic constituentist will say that the only difference between the two haecceities is that the former has Socrates plugged into the *is identical with* relation, and the latter has Plato. The *sui generis* constituentist will say that the only difference between the two haecceities is the former has Socrates plugged into the *sui generis* abstract object *being identical with x*, and the latter has Plato. In each case, there is a common element shared by each haecceity. According to the primitivist, there is no such common element. Both are haecceities, but they are primitive properties that don't share structure. The constituentist can make sense of there being a common element between haecceities.

A fourth reason to prefer constituentism to primitivism is that constituentism can make sense out of our ability to grasp haecceities of ordinary objects around us. As we noted in Chapter 1, there is some concern as to whether we have the ability to grasp many of the haecceities that exist. For instance, primitivist Gary Rosenkrantz thinks that we are not able to grasp haecceities of the ordinary objects that are around us. But if haecceities of objects around us have those objects as constituents, then we have a path to explaining how we can grasp these haecceities. The constituentist will say that the haecceity of my desk, *being my desk*, has my desk as a constituent. I am perceptually acquainted with my desk. As a result, why wouldn't I be able to grasp its haecceity? If haecceities have objects that instantiate them as constituents of them, then we may avoid the skepticism about grasping haecceities that we find in Rosenkrantz and in Roderick Chisholm in *Person and Object*. We will take up this issue further in Chapter 6.

A last strength of constituentism over primitivism rests on considerations of there being no necessary connections between distinct existences. Suppose that one followed Robert Adams in thinking that haecceities are dependent for their existence on the objects that instantiate them. (Presumably the no necessary connection problem doesn't arise with necessarily existing entities.) Consider then Socrates and his haecceity, *being Socrates*. If primitivism about haecceities is correct, then we have a necessary connection between two distinct contingent existences: Necessarily, Socrates exists only if *being Socrates* does. Some would find this necessary connection between distinct existences objectionable. Suppose, however, that constituentism is correct. Then, Socrates is a part of his haecceity, *being Socrates*. As a result, we don't really have a necessary connection between distinct objects. There is no more of a problem of a necessary connection with Socrates and his haecceity than there is with Socrates and singular propositions about him, or Socrates and his singleton.

38 The Nature of Haecceity

Thus, there are many reasons to prefer constituentism to primitivism. We turn now to consideration of some of the objections to constituentism.

2.2.2.2 Objections to Constituentism

In this section, we will consider a number of objections to constituentism. I will argue that none are insurmountable for the constituentist.

A first objection to constituentism proceeds as follows. The constituentist thinks that an haecceity like *being Mark Twain* has the author Mark Twain as a constituent. Then, the haecceity *being Mark Twain* will be identical with the haecceity *being Samuel Clemens*. But then, one can deduce *a priori* that Mark Twain=Samuel Clemens. But we can't deduce this *a priori*.

There are two things that the constituentist can say in reply to this objection. First, the primitivist presumably will have the same problem with *being Mark Twain* and *being Samuel Clemens*. For the primitivist, *being Mark Twain=being Samuel Clemens*. Haecceities aren't individuated any more finely than are objects, so an attempt to introduce intensionality with haecceities alone will fail. This is why Fregeans don't typically accept the idea that proper names express haecceities.[7] Haecceities simply are unable to do the work that Fregean senses are supposed to do.

Setting aside our first *tu quoque* response, the constituentist may give the same sort of reply to the objection that any direct reference theorist gives to problems of opacity. There are a wide number of such replies. For instance, she might adopt an idea of Nathan Salmon's [120] and say that there are non-semantically relevant modes of presentation through which we grasp haecceities, and these explain why we might not assent to the claim that Mark Twain=Samuel Clemens. Thus, I don't think the constituentist is any worse off here than is a direct reference theorist in similar contexts.

A second objection to constituentism centers on the idea of an individual being a constituent of an haecceity. The slot-theoretic constituentist thinks that individuals are "plugged into" the *is identical with* relation. The *sui generis* constituentist thinks that an individual is part of or plugged into the abstract function *being identical with x*. What precisely does this mean? How does this make sense? Gary Rosenkrantz puts the objection as follows:

> How does *a* [a random concrete object] a *concrete entity* "plug into" the Identity relation, an *abstract entity*? "Plugging" is not any intuitive or familiar relation which holds between properties and relations and *concreta*...Furthermore, the notion that an *abstract* entity has a *concrete* entity as a logical constituent or ingredient appears to be unintelligible ([117], p. 116).

But "plugging" concreta into abstracta isn't entirely unfamiliar; we have it in the case of singular propositions with concrete objects as constituents.

The Nature of Haecceity   39

And though the proposition itself isn't a property or relation (though it might be thought of as a 0-place relation), it is built up out of them. If we are able to understand a concrete object being a constituent of a singular proposition, we should be able to understand a concrete object being a constituent of an haecceity. In both instances, there are "slots" in the abstract object that are filled or "plugged" with concrete objects. (Indeed, we might think of the haecceity as a singular property.) As the notion of a singular proposition is coherent, I submit the notion of an haecceity with a concrete constituent also is coherent.

The next two objections to constituentism stem from the fact that haecceities with contingently existing concrete objects as constituents would themselves seem to exist contingently. (We will challenge this inference in a bit.)

The third objection to constituentism centers on the fact that an important use of haecceities is to serve as semantic contents of proper names and other rigid terms (Lockwood [84], Plantinga [101]). Why opt for haecceities rather than referents of rigid terms as semantic contents of the rigid terms? One reason is because the rigid term might be empty, and as a result, it would lack a semantic content. For someone like Plantinga [105], the haecceity exists whether or not the referent of the term exists, and thus, we have semantic contents for empty terms. But if a concrete individual is a constituent of its haecceity, then haecceities can't serve this semantic role.

Let us for now grant the assumption that haecceities with contingently existing constituents exist contingently. Is haecceities' utility as contents of rigid terms thereby undercut? Perhaps. If the reason why one wanted haecceities to be semantic contents of rigid terms is to avoid cases where the empty term had no content, and the proposed contents themselves existed just in case the referent of the rigid term did, then one would have no reason to adopt haecceities as contents. Of course, one might have other reasons for thinking that haecceities existed. (We will discuss this in the next chapter.) But the objection seems to have force if haecceities are as contingent as the references of the rigid terms, and giving semantic contents for empty terms is a prime desideratum of our theory of haecceity. Thus, if one accepts that haecceities with contingent constituents are themselves contingent, and it is important that haecceities serve as semantic contents of empty rigid terms, then one will feel pressure to give up constituentism. Of course, if one is a direct reference theorist (as I am), this problem doesn't arise.[8]

The fourth objection to constituentism arises from the constituentist's general claim that gerundial phrases with proper names in them often have as contents properties with concrete individuals in them. However, there are gerundial phrases with proper names where the name is empty, like "being jollier than Santa." What sort of property is *being jollier than Santa* for the constituentist? How could there exist such a property if Santa doesn't exist? (Suppose for the sake of argument assume that fictional names aren't successfully referring terms, *pace* philosophers like Thomasson [131] and Van Inwagen [136].)

At this point, the constituentist might avail herself of the same sorts of replies that a direct reference theorist employs to deal with cases of empty rigid terms. In particular, the constituentist might employ non-semantic modes of presentation along with a metaphysics of gappy properties to explain why it might seem that a particular gerundial phrase expresses a property (e.g. Braun ([21], [22]); Salmon [120], Soames [125]).

There is another solution for the constituentist in replying to both the third and fourth objections, however. That is to adopt what I have called elsewhere *independence actualism*.[9] Independence actualism is the thesis that although there are no nonexistent objects in the scope of our widest quantifiers, objects that don't exist may nevertheless exemplify some properties and stand in some relations.[10] For our purposes here, the independence actualist may allow that contingently existing concrete objects serve as constituents of propositions and properties even in worlds where the concrete object doesn't exist.[11] The concrete object may stand in the requisite propositional or property constituenthood relations even though it doesn't exist. Thus, haecceities may exist necessarily even if their constituents don't. This allows her, if she wants, to hold onto necessarily existing haecceities which can serve as semantic contents of empty names. Independence actualism also allows the constituentist to have haecceities of objects that don't exist. So, the constituentist independence actualist has a reply to our last two objections to constituentism.

Thus, I think that there are at least three things that the constituentist can say in reply to the last two objections to constituentism. These are not mutually exclusive strategies; the constituentist may adopt elements of more than one of them. First, she might give up the idea that haecceities are semantic contents of empty rigid terms. Second, she might avail herself of the sorts of tactics a direct reference theorist like Nathan Salmon or Scott Soames employs for dealing with empty terms. Third, she might adopt independence actualism and claim that haecceities are necessary existents, though their concrete constituents are not.

2.2.3 Slot-Theoretic Constituentism vs. Sui Generis Constituentism

To this point in the chapter, I have set out why I believe partism isn't a viable option as to the nature of haecceity, and I have given reasons to prefer constituentism to primitivism. I have not yet argued for *sui generis* constituentism over slot-theoretic constituentism. We turn to that now.

The slot-theoretic constituentist thinks that one gets the haecceity *being Socrates* by plugging Socrates into the relation *is identical with*. The *sui generis* constituentist believes you start with a *sui generis* abstract object, *being identical with x* and plug Socrates into it. Why prefer one to the other?

The most straightforward reason to prefer *sui generis* to slot-theoretic constituentism is that one finds slot theory objectionable, perhaps for the reasons one finds in Dixon [51] or Fine [53]. I myself *don't* find slot theory *per se* objectionable, primarily because I see no problem with multiplying things in the world that explain the instantiation of relations ("completions", as Fine calls them). But if one did find slot theory problematic, then one would have a reason to prefer *sui generis* to slot-theoretic constituentism.

The main reason I opt for *sui generis* over slot-theoretic constituentism centers on the ability of the former to explain facts that are brute on slot-theoretic constituentism. There are two such facts. The first is that on *sui generis* constituentism, we have an explanation of why it's impossible that things other than Socrates exemplify Socrates' haecceity. On *sui generis* constituentism, when Socrates is a constituent of his haecceity, there is no "room" for anything else to be a constituent. The gap in the *sui generis* abstract object is filled. Thus, we have some sort of account as to why nothing other than Socrates can exemplify *being Socrates*.

On slot-theoretic constituentism, we don't have a further account as to why things other than Socrates can't exemplify Socrates' haecceity. The slot-theoretic constituentist takes the haecceity *being Socrates* to be a partially saturated identity relation. There is no further reason why something other than Socrates can't exemplify such a property.[12]

There is a second advantage for *sui generis* constituentism that is related to its first. The *sui generis* constituentist has an account as to why an haecceity like *being Socrates* can't be multiply exemplified at a time. For a *sui generis* constituentist, the gap in the *sui generis* abstract object is filled with Socrates and thus can't be filled with anything else (any more than Socrates can be multiply located at a time). The slot-theoretic constituentist thinks that the haecceity *being Socrates* is structurally like any other property in having an open slot that is filled by a thing that exemplifies it. In this, *being Socrates* is like *being red*; both contain a slot that is filled by the thing that exemplifies the property. Yet, *being red* can be exemplified by multiple things at a time, and *being Socrates* cannot. That this is so is a primitive fact for the slot-theoretic constituentist.[13]

We should note, however, that the *sui generis* constituentist has her primitives as well. In the context of this discussion, we may note it is a primitive fact for her that multiple objects can't fit in a single slot in the abstract object *being identical with x*. This primitive seems preferable, however, to that of the slot-theoretic constituentist, because some properties with open slots may be exemplified by distinct things, and other properties can't.

Thus, I think that we have some reason to opt for *sui generis* over slot-theoretic constituentism. I've argued that we have strong reason to prefer some sort of constituentism to partism or primitivism. In the rest of the book, I take *sui generis* constituentism to be the correct view of the nature of haecceity. However, I will note those places where different conceptions of haecceity would have bearing on the course of argumentation.

In the next chapter, we take up questions of the rationale for believing in haecceities. What sorts of arguments are there for believing in haecceities? Or, why might one think that there *aren't* any such things?

Notes

1 That role is: an haecceity of an object x is that entity which explains the entelechy or thingness of x, and/or explains x's distinctness from all other objects.
2 It's not clear why their being primitive precludes their being qualitative. Perhaps the idea is that a qualitative haecceity would be something like a conjunction of qualitative properties. Robert Adams considers and rejects this view of haecceity; see Section 3.1 for discussion.
3 Daly [36] argues something similar with respect to tropes.
4 See Davidson [46] for discussion of souls with and without parts.
5 Here I will stipulate that colors exist on surfaces of physical objects and not on/in sense data; nothing of consequence for the discussion here rides on this. I'm also assuming there are surfaces; again nothing rests on this assumption, either.
6 For an excellent discussion of these issues, see Van Cleve [135].
7 Plantinga accepts the idea in 1974 in *The Nature of Necessity*, but he gives it up in "The Boethian Compromise" from 1978 in favor of finer-grained semantic contents that do the work that Fregean senses are supposed to do [101, 106]. I discuss this in Davidson [40].
8 Of course, the direct reference theorist will still face questions about the contents of empty rigid terms. I discuss this in Davidson [47], ch. 3.
9 See Davidson [47] for an extended explication and defense of independence actualism.
10 It is equivalent to what Plantinga calls "frivolous actualism" (Plantinga 2003b, p. 179).
11 See Davidson [47], chs. 2 and 3 for more on this strategy.
12 Similarly, there is no further reason on a primitivist view why something other than Socrates can't exemplify *being Socrates*. Thus, this also constitutes a reason for *sui generis* constituentism over-and-against primitivism.
13 Similarly, there is no further reason on a primitivist view why multiple things can't exemplify *being Socrates*. Thus, this also constitutes a reason for *sui generis* constituentism over-and-against primitivism.

3 Haecceity
Arguments for and Against

In this chapter, we will consider arguments for and against the existence of haecceities. In the first half of the chapter, we will look at arguments for haecceities. We will spend time trying to get clear on the relations between different sorts of arguments that one finds in the haecceity literature. I will argue that some of the arguments for haecceities are successful. In the second half of the chapter, we will consider arguments against the existence of haecceities. Here too we will try to get clear on the relations between different sorts of arguments against haecceity that one finds in the haecceity literature. I will argue that none of the arguments are successful in showing that haecceity is a flawed metaphysical concept. I will thus conclude that we have justification for believing in haecceities.

3.1 Arguments for Haecceity

There are two categories of arguments for the existence of haecceities, what I call "individuative" and "semantic" arguments. In Section 3.1.1, we will examine individuative arguments, and in Section 3.1.2, we will examine semantic arguments.

3.1.1 *Individuative Arguments for Haecceity*

The classic arguments for haecceities are individuative arguments. There are two flavors of individuative arguments. On one sort of argument, it is claimed that an haecceity is required for an object to be an individual. Arguments of this sort are *individuative arguments from singleness*. On the other sort of argument, it is claimed that haecceities are required to explain how it is that two objects x and y are distinct. Arguments of this sort are *individuative arguments from distinctness*. Often, these two sorts of arguments are run together, though they are different sorts of arguments. To see this, suppose I'm pointing at my desk. Individuative arguments from singleness posit haecceity to explain that this (pointing at my desk) is an individual entity—that is, it has entelechy or thingness. Individuative arguments from distinctness posit haecceity to explain that this (pointing at my desk) is distinct from that (pointing at my chair, or another desk that looks just like my desk).

Let's first consider the concept of individuative arguments from singleness, before turning our attention to individuative arguments from distinctness. The latter include the best-known arguments for the existence of haecceities.

3.1.1.1   Individuative Arguments from Singleness

The individuative arguments for haecceities in contemporary times have been arguments from distinctness. Scotus himself, however, seems to have been concerned primarily with questions of singleness, rather than with questions of distinctness.[1] As we saw in Chapter 1, Scotus argues that other rival accounts of the individuality or thingness of objects fail, and as a result, we should adopt his theory of haecceity. We noted in Chapter 1 that Ockham's reply to Scotus had two parts. First, Ockham argued that Scotus was wrong in thinking that there was any sort of real common nature that was held by distinct individuals of a particular type. Second, Ockham claimed that objects were self-individuating. There was nothing further needed to make Socrates an individual; he just was one.

The dialectic between Scotus and Ockham is instructive for thinking about individuative arguments from singleness. It is very difficult for me to see how a convincing individuative argument from singleness could be mounted against someone who accepted Ockham's view of individuals. Suppose someone like Scotus maintained that we need haecceity to explain the singleness or thingness of Socrates. The Ockhamist would retort that Socrates is a thing all by himself, and we need no further explanation of this fact. We'd then be at an impasse.

This inevitable impasse may account for the fact that we don't see defenders of haecceity after Scotus giving individuative arguments from singleness for haecceity.[2] Instead, their individuative arguments are from distinctness. These arguments, at least *prima facie*, have a better shot at convincing an interlocutor. We turn to them now.

3.1.1.2   Individuative Arguments from Distinctness

Any individuative argument from distinctness will posit an haecceity to explain that two objects A and B are distinct. The relations that A and B bear to each other may differ in at least three ways. First, A and B may exist at the same time but in different places; we will call these *synchronic* arguments from distinctness.[3] Second, A and B may exist at different times;

we will call these *diachronic* arguments from distinctness.[4] Third, A and B may exist in different worlds; we will call these *transworld* arguments from distinctness. The sorts of thought experiments that are typically used in individuative arguments from distinctness go back at least to Kant in the *Critique of Pure Reason* (A263, B319) and were revived in the 20th century by Max Black. These classic thought experiments involve two qualitatively exactly similar objects (droplets of water for Kant and iron spheres for Black) that exist simultaneously in different places.

The two most prominent examples of individuative arguments from distinctness in the haecceity literature are from Robert Adams and Gary Rosenkrantz. I want to consider the form of each of their distinctness arguments for haecceity here. I will argue that neither offer good arguments for the existence of haecceities because each fails to rule out a position like that of Ockham about individuation.

a. Robert Adams

In "Primitive Thisness and Primitive Identity," Robert Adams defends all three of the above sorts of arguments from distinctness (synchronic, diachronic, and transworld) for the existence of haecceities.[5] Adams' paper contains perhaps the best-known arguments for the existence of haecceities. In this section, we will consider his five principal arguments. I will argue that each suffers from the same sort of flaw–that none gives us reason to suppose a position like Ockham's about individuation cannot work.

Adams' first—and perhaps most-discussed—argument for the existence of haecceities is a synchronic argument involving qualitative exactly similar spheres (of the sort first proposed in Max Black's "The Identity of Indiscernibles" (Black [18])).

> We are to imagine a universe consisting solely of two large, solid globes of iron. They always have been, are, and always will be exactly similar in shape (perfectly spherical), size, chemical composition, color-in short, in every qualitative respect. They even share all their relational suchnesses [purely qualitative properties]; for example, each of them has the property of being two diameters from another iron globe similar to itself. Such a universe seems to be logically possible; hence, it is concluded that there could be two qualitatively indiscernible things and that the Identity of Indiscernibles is false (Adams [4], p. 13).

Call this first argument *the globe argument*. Of Adams' five arguments, we will spend the most time with this argument. His other arguments have a similar overall structure to the globe argument; criticisms of the globe argument will have applications to the other four arguments.

We should note the explicit conclusion of Adams' globe argument. It is that it is possible that there be distinct things that are qualitatively the same. Here and elsewhere in the paper, Adams believes that this is enough to show that there are or could be haecceities. Why is this? It is because Adams assumes that necessarily, each object o has the property *being identical with* o. The question for Adams, then, is whether *being identical with* o is itself identical with something like a maximal conjunction of o's qualitative properties (suchnesses), or rather is itself a primitive property. Adams thinks that if he can show that there can be two objects A and B that have all the same qualitative properties, then the properties *being identical with* A and *being identical with* B cannot be a maximal conjunction of qualitative properties. Thus, *being identical with* A and *being identical with* B must be primitive. That is, there must (possibly) be haecceities.

We can represent his reasoning in the globe argument more rigorously as follows.[6]

1. Necessarily, for any object o, o exemplifies the property *being identical with* o.
2. Necessarily, for any object o, the property *being identical with* o serves to individuate o from all other objects.
3. It is possible there be two distinct objects, A and B, that share all the same qualitative properties.
4. Therefore, it is possible A has the property *being identical with* A, and this property serves to individuate A from B (1,2,3).
5. Necessarily, for any object o1 and o2 and property P; if P serves to individuate o1 from o2; then P cannot be exemplified by both o1 and o2.
6. Therefore, it is possible *being identical with* A is had by A and not B (4,5).
7. Necessarily, for any object o, the property *being identical with* o is either a primitive haecceity or a maximal conjunction of qualitative properties.
8. If *being identical with* A were a maximal conjunction of qualitative properties, A and B would both exemplify *being identical with* A (3).
9. Therefore, it is possible *being identical with* A is a primitive haecceity (6,7,8).
10. Therefore, it is possible there are primitive haecceities (9).

Thus, Adams' argument assumes that necessarily every object o has a thisness (the property *being identical with* o), and we can show that the thisnesses involved in a scenario like that involving the two globes are primitive.

By way of evaluating this argument, consider what someone like Ockham would say about a case like that of Adams' iron globes. For someone like Ockham, the two globes are primitively distinct individuals. They aren't individuated by a further entity that one has and the other lacks. Then, what individuates the spheres? They just are individuated; it's a truly primitive fact that the spheres are distinct. They are self-individuating, as it were.[7]

We then shouldn't assume from the outset that there has to be some sort of entity like the property *being identical with this sphere* that serves to individuate the spheres, and our task is to discover the nature of this property. For someone who takes individuation to be truly brute, no such property is needed for individuation.[8]

The metaphysician who thinks that individuation is brute will reject (2), or perhaps (1) and (2) together. If individuation is brute, one could say that the property *being identical with o* doesn't individuate *o* from other objects (thus denying (2)). If we deny (2), we can't use (5) to arrive at (6) where *A* has a property *B* lacks. We need that *A* has a property *B* lacks to rule out *is identical with o* being the same as a maximal qualitative conjunction.

Or, if individuation is brute one could deny that there is a property named with "being identical with o" (thus denying (1)) and then go on to take as a result of this that *being identical with o* doesn't do any work in individuating *o* [thus denying (2)].

We can grant that Adams is right in thinking that his globe example shows that there can be distinct entities with all the same qualitative properties. However, there is no valid route from this claim to the claim that there are primitive haecceities before one rejects a view on which individuation is wholly brute. At most, Adams' globe argument yields a disjunction of a view that includes primitive haecceities and a truly primitive view about individuation.

Adams' second argument for the existence of haecceities is a diachronic argument involving qualitatively exactly similar events at different times.

> An argument for the possibility of non-identical indiscernibles, very similar to the argument from spatial dispersal, and as good, can also be given from *temporal* dispersal. For it seems that there could be a perfectly cyclical universe in which each event was preceded and followed by infinitely many other events qualitatively indiscernible from itself. Thus, there would be distinct but indiscernible *events*, separated by temporal rather than spatial distances (Adams [4], p. 14).

Call this second, diachronic, argument, *the argument from recurring events*. Suppose the looping event is the explosion of a firecracker on a concrete slab. Let E1 be one such event and E2 be the event after it. Both E1 and E2 are preceded by and followed by infinitely many events that are exactly like them: in either temporal direction we have infinitely many explosions of firecrackers. So we can't individuate E1 and E2 by the fact that they have different sorts of events that precede or follow them. Nevertheless, E1≠E2. The individuation must be done via some non-qualitative means, namely, a primitive haecceity.

Note that we can't appeal to the fact that the event that precedes E1 and the event that precedes E2 are distinct in our attempt to give a grounding that E1≠E2. Call the event before E1, "E1*." Then, we might be tempted to argue: The event that precedes E1 is E1*, the event that precedes E2 is E1. Thus via Leibniz's Law, E1≠E2. But we can see that we've just pushed the question of individuation back a step; we should now want to know what grounds the fact that E1*≠E1. The same issues that arose for accounting for the fact that E1≠E2 will arise in accounting for the fact that E1*≠E1.

Is the argument from recurring events for the existence of haecceities successful? One thing we should want to know in assessing it concerns the nature of time. Suppose that presentism is true. Then, it would seem that we *could* distinguish E1 from E2 without haecceities. Suppose E1 occurs at t1 and E2 occurs at t2. At t1, E1 has the property *being present* and E2 lacks this property. (This might be because wholly future entities lack all properties or because they have some properties but lack *being present*.) Thus at t1, E1≠E2. But of course, distinctness is necessary, so necessarily E1≠E2.

Suppose, however, that eternalism is true. Then, this second argument from Adams really is a temporal analog of the globe argument. E1 and E2 take up regions of spacetime that are qualitatively identical in their relations to all other regions of spacetime. But E1≠E2, and there must be primitive haecceities that explain this fact, Adams reasons.

Suppose then that we grant that eternalism is true for the sake of evaluating the argument from recurring events. This will allow Adams to avoid individuation of E1 and E2 by tensed properties. However, even granting eternalism, there still is a problem with Adams' argument. This is evident when we note that the role of the recurring events in this second argument is functionally the same as the iron globes in the globe argument. With the globe argument, we noted that his reasoning validly yielded only the disjunction of a view on which primitive haecceities individuate and an Ockhamist sort of view on which individuation is truly primitive. The same applies in the argument from recurring events. We may grant the possibility of there being distinct events that are qualitatively the same in their intrinsic and relational properties. However, Adams gives no argument that we need something further—primitive haecceities—to individuate the events. Without this, the reasoning in the argument from recurring events doesn't yield the conclusion Adams desires.

Adams' calls his third argument *the argument from the possibility of almost indiscernible twins*. Adams introduces the argument as follows:

No one doubts that there could be a universe like the universe of our example [with the iron globes] in other respects, if one of the two globes had a small chemical impurity that the other lacked. Surely, we may think, the absence of the impurity would not make such a universe impossible (Adams [4], p. 17).

So far his reasoning serves as an adjunct to that in the globe argument. In the vein of this first case of nearly-indiscernible globes, he develops a new thought experiment to show that there can be distinct qualitatively exactly similar things.

Suppose I have an almost indiscernible twin. The only qualitative difference between him and me, and hence between his part of the universe and mine, is that on one night of our lives (when we are 27 years old) the fire-breathing dragon that pursues me in my nightmare has ten horns, whereas the monster in his dream has only seven...But if such a world is even possible, it seems to follow that a world with perfectly indiscernible twins is also possible. For surely I could have existed, and so could my twin, if my monster had had only seven horns, like his (Adams [4], pp. 17–18).

Adams' argument from the possibility of almost indiscernible twins then is a synchronic argument that is very much in the flavor of the globe argument. However, it faces hurdles that the globe argument doesn't. In particular, many think that the contents of some of one's mental states are determined in part by the environment in which one is situated.[9] In Adams' example, we are to imagine the near-twins each in a different "part of the universe." Suppose we take this to mean that the near-twins are spatially far distant from each other. Then, in the almost-indiscernible-twin case perhaps we don't have near psychological duplicates that differ only in numbers of dragon horns. Mental semantic externalism then would seem to threaten this argument of Adams'.

There are three replies to this criticism that I could imagine Adams making. First, Adams might concede that the argument from recurring events won't work. However, he has four other arguments that there are primitive haecceities. He could contend that the case for his main conclusion is overdetermined and isn't affected by this particular argument being shown to be problematic.

Second, Adams might try to modify or clarify his initial example by putting the near-twins in the same environment. Adams' statement of the argument might suggest that the near-twins are far away from each other. But there's no reason why the twins couldn't be in close-enough proximity (if necessary, for their entire lives) to where the wide contents of their thoughts would line up. Then, we could have people whose thoughts really did differ only in terms of numbers of dragon horns.

Third, Adams might question either the truth or the necessity of mental semantic externalism. The arguments for it are not apodictic. And, even if one is convinced by the sorts of thought experiments used in arguments for mental semantic externalism, one might hold that they establish only that it holds in nearby worlds. For instance, we are to imagine a world in which individuals have different stuff playing the watery role in their environments (H_2O and XYZ). The contents of their watery thoughts differ. But perhaps that is just in nearby worlds; perhaps there are far-off worlds in which two such individuals in different watery environments would have watery thoughts of the same contents. I am inclined to think that the reasoning in the thought experiments that get us to mental externalism establishes it as a necessary truth, but perhaps it doesn't.

We can see, then, that the case Adams considers in the argument from almost indiscernible twins introduces complexities not found in the original globe case. However, even if Adams can rescue this third argument, it too will face the same sort of problem that the globe argument faced. There we saw that there is an inference from the possibility of qualitatively exactly similar globes to the existence of primitive haecceities that serve to individuate the globes. We noted that Adams fails to rule out a truly primitive view like that of Ockham's. The argument from almost indiscernible twins faces the same difficulty. Even if we are able to get from the two humans with only slightly different dreams to two qualitatively exactly similar humans, we need an argument that their individuation requires primitive haecceities. We don't get that from Adams. As before, it's very difficult to see how such an argument would go. Thus, the argument from almost indiscernible twins fails as an argument for the existence of haecceities.

We will consider Adams' last two arguments together. Each is a transworld argument that identity across possible worlds requires primitive haecceities.

We will call Adams' fourth argument *the Castor-Pollox argument*. Adams imagines a world $w1$ where there are two qualitatively exactly similar globes, one named "Castor" and other other "Pollox." In $w1$, each of them always exists. Adams then gives the rest of the argument:

> But it seems perfectly possible, both logically and metaphysically, that either or both of them cease to exist. Let $w2$ then, be a possible world just like $w1$ up to a certain time t at which in $w2$ Castor ceases to exist while Pollux goes on forever; and let $w3$ be a possible world just like $w2$ except that in $w3$ it is Pollux that ceases to exist at t while Castor goes on forever...[T]here is no qualitative difference between $w2$ and $w3$.

And there are no qualitative necessary and sufficient conditions for the transworld identity or non-identity of Castor and Pollox; for every qualitative condition satisfied by Castor in $w2$ is satisfied by Pollux in $w1$, and vice versa (Adams [4], p. 22).

Adams' fifth and final argument for primitive haecceities comes immediately after his fourth. It builds on his fourth argument:

A similar example can be constructed for transworld identity of *events*. Suppose all that happens in $w1$ is that Castor and Pollux approach and recede from each other in an infinite series of indiscernible pulsations of the universe. In $w1$ their pulsations go on forever, but they might not have. For every pair of them there is surely a possible world in which one member of the pair is the last pulsation and a different possible world in which the other is the last pulsation. But there is no qualitative difference between these possible worlds...There are therefore no qualitative necessary and sufficient conditions for the transworld identities and non-identities of the events in these possible worlds (Adams [4], p. 23).

Call this fifth argument *the Castor-Pollux pulsation argument*. With both the Castor-Pollux argument and the Castor-Pollux pulsation argument, there are no qualitative necessary and sufficient conditions that would ground transworld identity. This implies that no haecceity can be qualitative: in Adams' terminology that no thisness is a suchness. Thus, the haecceity must be primitive.

We now see immediately that these arguments are flawed. Suppose we concede that there are no qualitative differences between $w1$ and $w2$ and that the only differences between the two worlds are with respect to identities. (This would be to say that *haecceitism* is true.)[10] It doesn't follow that haecceities are necessary to ground the identities between the entities in different worlds. As before, it may be that the identities are truly primitive. It might be that it is a brute fact that this thing in $w1$ is identical with that thing in $w2$. The grounding of transworld identity *could*, of course, be done by haecceities. But to establish that individuation *has* to be by haecceity one needs to foreclose on the Ockhamist option. Adams doesn't do this. As before, it is very difficult to see how he could.

At the end of the "Primitive Thisness and Primitive Identity," Adams summarizes what he has tried to show:

I have argued that there are possible cases in which no purely qualitative conditions would be both necessary and sufficient for possessing a given thisness (Adams [4], p. 24).

From this, one might otherwise think that Adams isn't trying to show that there are haecceities. Rather, he is just trying to show that they don't supervene in a strong sense on qualitative conditions or properties. (That is, that haecceitism is true.) But he *is* trying to show that there are haecceities. We can see this if we consider what he says two years later in the paper "Actualism and Thisness." There, Adams summarizes what he believes himself to have demonstrated in "Primitive Thisness and Primitive Identity."

> I have argued elsewhere [in "Primitive Thisness and Primitive Identity"] that thisness holds a place beside suchness as a fundamental feature of reality (Adams [5], p. 3).

> A thisness, in the sense intended here, is the property of being a particular individual or of being identical with that individual...I have argued [in Primitive Thisness and Primitive Identity] that there could be thisnesses that would not be equivalent to any purely qualitative property and that thisnesses are therefore primitive in the sense of being in principle distinct from all purely qualitative properties (Adams [5], p. 4).

Adams takes himself to be arguing that the world contains a certain type of entity—primitive haecceities or thisnesses. The opponent of Adams in "Primitive Thisness and Primitive Identity" is Leibniz, who thinks there are no primitive haecceities and all properties are qualitative. Leibniz is committed to the identity of indiscernibles.[11] Thus, Leibniz can be refuted if the identity of indiscernibles is rejected, and Adams does so in a series of thought experiments that we've examined above. But rejecting the identity of indiscernibles doesn't by itself establish that there are primitive haecceities. It does so only if one rejects entirely the possibility of distinct objects that share all the same properties. Someone who thinks that individuation is truly brute could take Adams' arguments against the identity of indiscernibles to be sound and still reject the proposition that there are primitive haecceities. Leibniz and the haecceity theorist disagree about the possibility of two objects sharing all the same qualitative properties. However, Leibniz and the haecceity theorist *agree* that there cannot be distinct objects that share all the same properties. The haecceity theorist simply expands the class of available properties to include non-qualitative haecceities. There is another possibility on the table here, one that agrees with Adams against Leibniz that there can be distinct objects that share all the same qualitative properties and goes on to reject the positing of non-qualitative haecceities to explain or ground the distinctness. This possibility remains at the conclusion of each of Adams' arguments that are intended to show that there are haecceities. Adams does nothing to rule out such a position. Thus, I conclude that Adams' arguments in his important "Primitive Thisness and

Primitive Identity," in spite of their billing, are not good individuative arguments from distinctness for haecceity. They establish at most only the disjunction of a view that involves haecceities and a truly brute individuative view like Ockham's.

Hacking and Diekemper on Adams-type Arguments

In a very interesting discussion of arguments against the identity of indiscernibles, Ian Hacking [62] criticizes arguments like those of Adams in "Primitive Thisness and Primitive Identity." In particular, Hacking argues that when one tries to describe a possible world like the one in Adams' globe argument, there is no fact of the matter as to whether there is one or two globes in the world. Hacking thinks that one is able to conclude that there are two globes if one assumes absolute spacetime, but to assume that spacetime in the world is absolute is question-begging against the defender of the identity of indiscernibles.

In his discussion of Hacking (Adams [4], pp. 14 ff.), Adams notes that an important question concerns the geometry of spacetime in the world in question. Suppose we describe the world as follows: If one begins in the center of a globe and travels 2 diameters of the globe from that point, one arrives at the center of a globe. If the world turned out to have two globes in it in a relatively flat spacetime, we could explain this fact. However, if there is one globe and spacetime is very curved, we also could begin in the center of a globe, travel 2 diameters of the globe, and arrive at the center of a globe.

In a more recent discussion of Hacking and Adams, Joseph Diekemper is sympathetic to Hacking's general line of reasoning against Adams-type arguments (Diekemper [49]). Diekemper agrees with Hacking that it is question-begging to assume absolute space holds of Adams' two-globe world (Diekemper [49], p. 269). Diekemper also argues that to assume that spacetime is not very curved in an Adams-type scenario is to beg the question against the objector to an Adams-type argument:

> [F]or all we know, whether a world is Euclidean or non-Euclidean might have everything to do with how many objects it contains; and if it does, then we will have begged the question...in assuming the two-sphere world is different from the one-sphere world in virtue of being Euclidean (Diekemper [49], p. 267).

One is able to arrive at the world of Adams' globe argument only if one assumes space is not relative and too curved. To make this assumption is tantamount begging the question against the defender of the identity of indiscernibles.

There are difficult issues here as to when giving a counterexample to a claim should be thought of as begging the question against the claim. If you believe p, and I offer the following counterexample to p: ¬p; well, that seems impermissible. In giving a counterexample to p, I should offer something q that entails ¬p and that itself is more obviously true than ¬p. But what if q is very close in plausibility to ¬p and clearly entails ¬p? Have I begged the question in such a case? It is true that if space is relative and very curved and we don't build in the claim that we have two globes, we aren't able to give a qualitative description of the world that entails there are two globes rather than one. But the person offering the counterexample to a claim is able to craft the counterexample the way she wants, so long as she isn't adding elements that make the example obviously incoherent. Suppose Hacking says in reply to Adams' globe world: "But what if space in your world is really curved and is relational? Then you have two globes only if you antecedently state there are two globes." Adams would be well within his rights to reply, "then in the world of my example space isn't relational and very curved." The curvature of space is, of course, a contingent matter. So, there should be no prohibition on Adams constructing his world without very curved space. The nature of spacetime—whether it is absolute or relational—would seem to be a matter of necessity. But neither option for the nature of space is obviously incoherent. If Adams can show there are primitive haecceities if one assumes there is absolute, relatively flat space, that's surely enough to give *prima facie* justification there could be haecceities. But I think Adams' position is better than this. Adams could grant that space is relational; so long as in the world in question, there are qualitatively exactly similar sphere(s) that are related to each other along a flat (enough) line to allow that there could be two globes. To insist that to construct either sort of counterexample is to beg the question surely is too much. The counterexamples are not obviously incoherent, and to insist that they are question-begging pushes one in the direction of saying any true counterexample to a claim p begs the question against the person who holds p. After all, if the example holds, p is false!

Imagine the following reply to Adams: "I'll grant that space is absolute and not too curved. But in your example you claim there are two globes. But what if there is just one globe that is located in two places at the same time? To insist that your example involves two globes rather than one bilocated one begs the question against the defender of the identity of indiscernibles." Adams ought to say, "I get to set the terms of the example, and I'm saying there are two globes rather than one that is bilocated.[12] That it entails the falsity of the identity of indiscernibles doesn't imply it begs the question. It just implies that it's a properly-constructed counterexample."

Thus, I don't think that Hacking and Diekemper show that Adams begs the question against someone like Leibniz in giving arguments like his globe argument. We turn now to a temporal individuative argument for haecceities from Joseph Diekemper. Diekemper claims that his argument allows him to avoid the problems that he believes that Adams' arguments invite.

b. Diekemper's Temporal Individuative Argument

Though Diekemper thinks that spatial individuative arguments from distinctness beg the question against the defender of the identity of indiscernibles, he does think that there is a successful temporal individuative argument from distinctness (Diekemper [49], pp. 269 ff.). In giving his argument, Diekemper asks us to imagine two different worlds. In the first—which we will call W_L—we are to imagine four event types: A, B, C, D. In W_L there is an infinite series of concrete events of these four types, occurring in order. Thus, at any point in time, there are infinitely many events of each type in one's future and past. Contrast W_L with a world W_C where there are four concrete events that recur in an infinite circular pattern (...A-B-C-D-A-B-C-D...). Diekemper believes that time in W_C must be B-theoretic:

> [A]ll events in a circular time series must be equally real. This follows because if each of the four events in the circular time series A B C D occurs once and only once, and there is no beginning to the series, then it is always the case that every event has occurred...I know of no more apt criterion for the reality of an event than its occurrence. So when event A is present to a subject, it is also the case that the very same event lies in the subject's past and future, and thus there can be no objective distinction between past, present, and future in circular time (Diekemper [49], p. 270).

Time in W_L, by contrast, need not be B-theoretic:

> Now consider linear repeating time. Clearly, it is conceivable that such a time series be static, but it should be just as clear that it is also conceivably...dynamic (Diekemper [49], p. 270).

> What we have discovered is that a circular world is necessarily static, while a repeating linear world is not, and that this difference determines a difference in ontology (Diekemper [49], p. 271).

Diekemper thinks then that W_C gives us a case where we have a counterexample to the identity of indiscernibles and thus a need for primitive haecceities to do work in individuation.

I think that there is a problem with Diekemper's argument for primitive haecceities, however. One might think from Diekemper's discussion that

56 Haecceity

W_C contains distinct events that are qualitatively the same. But it doesn't contain these. Rather, it contains the same four events that recur over time. Each of the four events in W_C are multiply located in different regions of spacetime. We aren't, then, faced with a case where we have this event A which is distinct from, though qualitatively the same as that event (also called) A. Rather, this event A *is identical with* that event A. That is, they aren't distinct and thus need nothing to explain their distinctness. Thus, we don't have in W_C either a counterexample to the identity of indiscernibles or part of an argument that there must be primitive haecceities in order to individuate.

We can see that this event A=that event A (and every event A) in the following passage:

> [A]lthough there is a sense in which the events in a circular time series continually repeat themselves, strictly speaking, each event occurs only once–given that each event is numerically identical to all of its "repetitions." Again, the type/token distinction can help clarify the distinction between [W_L and W_C]: both worlds contain only four event types, but [W_L] also contains an infinite number of tokens of those types; whereas [W_C] contains only four tokens–one corresponding to each type (Diekemper [49], pp. 269–270).

What if Diekemper gave up the identity of each event A and said that each concrete event A is distinct, though qualitatively exactly the same as every other concrete event A? If he did that, he'd have W_L, and in W_L he has no way to force a B-theory of time. As we've described things in W_L, time could be either A-theoretic or B-theoretic. If it is the former, we may see immediately that we won't have trouble with individuating this A-event from that A-event. At each moment in time there is at most one A-event.

But can't Diekemper just *stipulate* that time in W_L is B-theoretic? Perhaps, though perhaps not given the things that he says about Adams. If Diekemper were to stipulate that time in W_L is B-theoretic, he'd be building in the assumptions about the nature of time he needs to get the counterexample to the identity of indiscernibles he wants. But that's the sort of thing he faulted Adams for doing in Adams' arguments for primitive haecceities. If he thought Adams was begging the question with Adams' arguments, Diekemper would have to say the same thing about his own argument here, were he to stipulate that time in W_L is B-theoretic.

Now, this is a bit of a *tu quoque* response to Diekemper, especially since I argued in the last section that Adams doesn't beg the question in his individuative arguments for primitive haecceities. Let us then suppose that there would be no problems with begging the question were Diekemper to stipulate that time in W_L was B-theoretic. Were Diekemper to make this stipulation about time in W_L, he then would have distinct, qualitatively exactly similar events at different times. Then we would be faced with a question as to how this A-event is distinct from this other A-event at a different time. That is, Diekemper's argument would be an analog of Adams' argument from recurring events. As such, it would be subject to the same basic criticism, that is, it fails to rule out a metaphysics of individuation like that of Ockham.

c. Gary Rosenkrantz's Spatial Individuative Argument

In his 1993 book *Haecceity: An Ontological Essay*, Gary Rosenkrantz's main argument for the existence of haecceities is a synchronic individuative argument from distinctness. Rosenkrantz begins his main argument for the existence of haecceities with a variation of a one-over-many argument for Platonism. This argument is important for his main argument for haecceities in that it establishes the need for a property that makes particulars distinct.

Argument B

(B1) At a time, *t*, a particular *x* and a particular *y* are diverse.

(B2) There is something about *x* and *y* in virtue of which *x* is diverse from *y* at *t*.

(B3) This something [which explains the diversity of *x* and *y* at *t*] can only be that *x* has a property at *t* which *y* lacks at *t*.

Therefore,

(B4) A property exists (Rosenkrantz [117], p. 74).

For our purposes here (at the start of Rosenkrantz's overall argument for haecceities), (B3) is most important. If we have the truth of (B3), we then seek a property that explains or accounts for the diversity of distinct objects. Rosenkrantz thinks that (B3) is true; to find this property is to solve what he calls "the problem of individuation."

> The problem of accounting for the diversity of particulars at a time is traditionally known as *the problem of individuation*. To solve this problem one must discover an appropriate *principium individuatioinis* or *criterion of individuation*. An appropriate principle or criterion of individuation provides an analysis of the diversity of particulars at a time which is a logically necessary and sufficient explanation for the diversity of particulars at a time (Rosenkrantz [117], p. 75).

The criteria of individuation to which Rosenkrantz refers in the paragraph above is related to the property mentioned in (B3). In attempting to get at the nature of this property, Rosenkrantz seeks to fill in the right-hand side of the following biconditional schema with a property that x has and y lacks, or conversely:

At a time, t, a particular x is diverse from a particular y = df

Rosenkrantz devotes the lion's share of the second chapter of his book to sussing out a criterion of individuation that will complete the right-hand side of the biconditional. His argument is an argument by elimination. He considers a number of possibilities (which I will state in slightly less-difficult language than that which Rosenkrantz employs):

1 A material criterion: x and y at t are made of different portions of stuff.
2 A substratum criterion: x and y at t have different substrata.
3 A locational criterion: x and y at t are in different places.
4 A mereological criterion: x and y at t have different parts.
5 A causal criterion: x and y at t have different causes or effects.
6 A tropal criterion: x and y at t possess different tropes.
7 A relational criterion: x and y at t are related in some irreflexive way (e.g. are spatially distant).
8 An haecceity criterion: x and y at t possess different haecceities.

Rosenkrantz argues that 1–7 fail as criteria of individuation. It is not crucial for our purposes here that we work through the details of these arguments. It is sufficient to note that the recurring theme in his arguments against 1–7 is that the proposed individuator (places, parts, causes, etc.) itself needs individuation and thus can't properly individuate. (Rosenkrantz puts this point in the language of circularity.) Only the haecceity criterion is left standing as a criterion of individuation. Thus, it must be that x and y are distinct because x has the property *being x* and y lacks it, or y has the property *being y* and x lacks it (or both).

Why doesn't 8 fail for the same reason? Because haecceities are abstract objects and aren't themselves in need of (or capable of) individuation.

> The moral of this story is that an attempt to individuate a particular *qua* particular by relating it to another particular commits us to circular individuation...whereas trying to individuate a particular *qua* particular by relating it to an abstract object does not commit us to such circular individuation (Rosenkrantz [117], p. 103).

> [S]ince we have analyzed the diversity of *concreta* at a time by relating *concreta* to *abstracta*, we cannot also analyze the diversity of *abstracta* at a time by relating *abstracta* to *concreta*, on

pain of vicious circularity...And it was shown above that the diversity of *abstracta* at a time cannot be analyzed by relating *abstracta* to *abstracta*...Therefore, it seems that the diversity of *abstracta* at a time is an unanalyzable brute fact (Rosenkrantz [117], p. 135).

Thus, we have before us the structure of Rosenkrantz's individuative argument from distinctness for haecceity. Is it a good argument? A problem very similar to that which generated the central problem in Adams' globe argument appears in Rosenkrantz's argument. To see this, first consider again (B3):

(B3) This something can only be that x has a property at t which y lacks at t.

Only when we have (B3) are we are set on a quest to find an individuating property, a quest which terminates in haecceities. Clearly then, (B3) is an important step in Rosenkrantz's argument.

We reach (B3) after accepting (B2):

(B2) There is something about x and y in virtue of which x is diverse from y at t.

Suppose, however, that I think individuation is primitive in the way that Ockham does. Why would I accept the truth of (B2)? Someone like Ockham thinks that objects x and y *just are* individuated and that there is no further feature of them that grounds the distinctness of x and y. So, he wouldn't grant that there is anything (further, like a property) in virtue of which x and y are distinct. Thus, if I'm an Ockhamist about individuation, I have no reason to accept (B2). Maybe (B2) is correct, but to assert it without argument is to beg the question against someone like Ockham. If we don't have reason to accept (B2), we have no reason to conclude with (B3) that there must be a *property* that individuates x and y. If we don't have (B3), we have no reason to seek a reductive analysis of numerical diversity of the sort given in 1–8 above. And if we have no reason to seek a reductive analysis of numerical diversity as we have in 1–8, we don't land on the haecceity criterion as the one candidate left standing among principles of individuation. Thus, Rosenkrantz's main argument for the existence of haecceities is unsuccessful. It cannot succeed until a positive case is made against someone who follows Ockham's line about individuation. That is, it cannot succeed until we've reason to accept (B2).

It's worth noting that Rosenkrantz himself doesn't think that (B2) is a necessary truth when the variables range over all objects. (B2) holds for concrete objects only. As we've seen, for Rosenkrantz, abstract objects are self-individuating. The Ockhamist simply thinks that what Rosenkrantz believes about abstract objects holds of all objects.

3.1.1.3 Conclusion

In this section, we've examined several individuative arguments from distinctness—five from Robert Adams and one each from Joseph Diekemper and Gary Rosenkrantz. All of them have been seen to fail. Many of them fail in the same sort of way, *viz.*, that they fail to rule out a view on which individuation is truly brute. Indeed, it is very difficult to see how an argument ruling out this view might go without begging the question against someone like Ockham. In this, these individual arguments from distinctness are similar to the individual argument from singleness we considered at the start of the chapter.

I find it a striking result that none of the individuative arguments from distinctness work; the primary reason why philosophers believe in haecceities is the role they play in individuation.[13] If we seek a reason for accepting the existence of haecceities, we should consider a different sort of argument for them. We turn to our second class of arguments for haecceity, semantic arguments.

3.1.2 Semantic Arguments for Haecceity

Semantic arguments for haecceity turn on the claim that haecceities are needed to provide semantic contents of linguistic expressions or are needed for giving truth conditions to modal sentences.[14] I want to state and evaluate a number of semantic arguments for haecceity in this section.

A first semantic argument for the existence of haecceities is that they can serve as semantic contents of proper names. A number of philosophers have used haecceities to serve as the semantic contents of proper names (e.g. Lockwood [84], Plantinga [101]). Why might someone adopt a view on which names express haecceities, rather than, say, a direct reference view on which the semantic contents of names are their referents? The principal reason is that haecceities can serve as semantic contents of empty names. If I think that haecceities are necessary existents, then a name like "Vulcan" can have a semantic content—the haecceity *being Vulcan*—even though the name is empty. A second reason might stem from an aversion to Russellian singular propositions. If one were a primitivist about haecceities and thought that haecceities were constituents of propositions, one could avoid concrete objects as constituents of propositions.[15]

A second semantic argument for the existence of haecceities involves extending this idea to other rigid terms, such as indexicals (e.g. Chisholm, [25, 31]). So, terms like "I", "this", and "that" might be thought to express haecceities. The above motivations for having proper names express haecceities would apply here. In addition, one with Fregean intuitions might think that indexicals (rather than names) are particularly suited to have haecceities as semantic contents, as names are the sorts of things that are more likely to have senses or modes of presentation as part of their semantic contents.[16]

I am inclined to accept direct reference about the contents of rigid terms, and as a result, I am not drawn to haecceities via their use as semantic contents for these terms. But for those who do find a use for haecceities in giving contents of rigid terms, this will serve for them as a reason for thinking there are haecceities.

A third semantic argument for haecceities is that they serve as semantic contents of quidditative predicates like "is Socrates" or "is identical with this desk." The argument is straightforward. Suppose we think that sentences express propositions that serve as the semantic contents of the sentences. Suppose further we think that the proposition has constituents that are the semantic contents of parts of the sentence that expresses the proposition. The semantic contents of well-formed predicates are properties. Thus, the semantic contents of quidditative predicates like "is Socrates" and "is identical with this desk" are properties that are part of the proposition expressed by sentences in which they appear. The only sort of properties that these predicates might express are haecceities. Thus, there are haecceities.

There are places to resist this argument, though I find it compelling. One might object to the claim that propositions have constituents, as Trenton Merricks [96] does, or that their constituents are the semantic values of the parts of the sentences that express them. One might also object to the claim that the semantic values of predicates are properties or to the claim that haecceities are the only candidates for properties that quidditative predicates express. Or, one might object to the claim that only existing properties may serve as semantic contents of linguistic items. But all of these claims look evidently true to me, and thus, I think the semantic argument for haecceities from the semantic contents of quidditative predicates is very powerful. Indeed, I think it's our strongest reason for believing in haecceities. It is a much better argument for the existence of haecceities than the well-known individuative arguments for them.

A fourth semantic argument for haecceities is that they serve as referents of quidditative gerundial phrases like "being Socrates" or "being this desk." Here is Alvin Plantinga in "World and Essence" making this sort of case:

> Indeed, is there any reason to suppose that "being identical with Socrates" names a property? Well, is there any reason to suppose that it does not?...Surely it is true of Socrates that he is Socrates and that he is identical with Socrates. If those are true

of him, then *being Socrates* and *being identical with Socrates* characterize him; they are among his properties or attributes (Plantinga [110], p. 58).

It's not clear to me that we should think of Plantinga here as doing more than merely *asserting* that "being identical with Socrates" names a property. But perhaps this is the most one can hope for with semantic arguments for haecceities that take them to be referents of quidditative gerundial phrases. We note that there are meaningful, well-formed quidditative gerundial phrases, and we infer that they must refer to haecceities.

There are the seeds of a fifth semantic argument for haecceities in Plantinga's remarks, however. Consider first a straightforward one-over-many type argument from similarity for the existence of a property: This car, that door, and this book all have in common something; the attribute *being red*. We then might give a similar argument from difference between objects: This car and that door have something that is different between them, the attribute *being made of wood*. Suppose then I point at Socrates and Plato: These individuals have something that is different between them, the attribute *being Socrates*. Thus, one may arrive at the existence of haecceities in much the same way that one might arrive at the existence of other properties.

Now, there are many objections to these sorts of one-over-many arguments, objections that stretch back to their origination in Plato. If one is inclined to think that they are good arguments (perhaps in a souped-up form, as we see from Peter van Inwagen ([138], chs. 3, 4, 8)) as I am, then one will be inclined to accept haecceities.

Finally, a sixth semantic argument for haecceities comes from the utility of haecceities in giving truth conditions for modal sentences. Suppose one is an actualist; that one thinks that necessarily there are no nonexistent objects.[17] It might then be difficult to see how to flesh out a metaphysics from the Kripke semantics for modal logic. On the Kripke semantics, in addition to there being a set of objects that is the domain of objects in a particular possible world, there also is a union of all the objects in all possible worlds. There are objects in this union that don't exist at the actual world, α. We then seem to be committed to its being true at α that there are things that don't exist. This contradicts actualism. The Kripke semantics provide deep insight into modality; thus it would be nice to be able to square metaphysics drawn from the Kripke semantics with actualism.

Alvin Plantinga has done exactly this in a series of works (see essays in Plantinga [108]), particularly in "Actualism and Possible Worlds." Plantinga proposes using necessarily existing haecceities to stand in for nonexistent objects. These haecceities will allow him to give truth conditions for modal sentences that would otherwise seem to commit us to there being nonexistent objects. To see how this would work, consider the sentence,

(S1) There could have been an object that doesn't actually exist.

(S1) is true in the actual world, α. From the Kripke semantics, one would give the following truth conditions to (S1): (S1) is true at α just if there is an object x in the union of domains of objects across all worlds, such that x doesn't exist at α but does exist at another possible world W. On this account, the union of all possible objects is doing truthmaking work at α. This seems to say that there are things that don't exist at α, which violates actualism. Plantinga, however, gives an alternate semantics using haecceities for sentences like (S1). For Plantinga, (S1) is true in α just if there is an haecceity that is not instantiated in α but is instantiated in another world, W. [18] Haecceities exist necessarily for Plantinga, so in α there are haecceities that aren't instantiated in α. The haecceity thus does the work (or something like the work) that the nonexistent object did in our initial gloss of (S1).

This is an ingenious use of haecceities in maintaining actualism while embracing the metaphysics that flows from the Kripke semantics for modal logic. There has been a great deal written about Plantinga's haecceitistic semantics, with some arguing that it fails to assign some truth conditions correctly (Menzel [93], McMichael [92], Linsky/Zalta [83]); and others helping to explain and extend it (Jager [73]). I myself have argued that one can maintain actualism and deny that there are necessarily existing haecceities if one embraces a strategy of allowing objects that don't exist to exemplify properties and stand in relations (Davidson [47], ch. 3). If I am right, one can avoid haecceities in giving an actualistic semantics for modal sentences. But if one agrees with Alan McMichael [92] in thinking that one needs either nonexistent objects or haecceities to adequately give truth conditions for modal sentences, then we have a successful sixth semantic argument for the existence of haecceities.

We have before us six semantic arguments for the existence of haecceities, then. By my lights, at least two of them are good arguments. Thus, though the best-known arguments for haecceities—individuative arguments—fail; nevertheless, it seems to me we have a *prima facie* case for accepting the existence of haecceities.

To determine if we have *ultima facie* reasons for believing in haecceities, we must also examine arguments *against* the existence of haecceities. We turn to consideration of those now.

3.2 Arguments against Haecceity

In this section, I want to state and critique a number of objections to haecceities that one finds in the haecceity literature.

3.2.1 The Triviality Objection

The first objection to haecceities is that they are trivial in some objectionable way. A statement of it may be found in Max Black's classic dialogue "The Identity of Indiscernibles."

> A. How will this do for an argument? If two things, a and b, are given, the first has the property of being identical with a. Now b cannot have this property, for else b would be a, and we should have only one thing, not two as assumed. Hence, a has at least one property, which b does not have, that is to say the property of being identical with a.
>
> B. This is a round about way of saying nothing, for "a has the property of being identical with a" means no more than "a is a". When you begin to say "a is ..." I am supposed to know what thing you are referring to as "a" and I expect to be told something about that thing. But when you end the sentence with the words "...is a" I am left still waiting. The sentence "a is a" is a useless tautology (Black [18], p. 11).

Interlocutor A suggests that Black's spheres differ in haecceities; only one of them has the haecceity *being identical with a*. Interlocutor B claims that the property *being identical with a* is trivial. But what exactly is the problem that Interlocutor B claims to see with individuation by haecceity? There are two potential objections here, I take it. First, B says that to claim *a* exemplifies *being identical with a* is to say the same thing as that *a*=*a*. But that doesn't seem to be right, for even people who reject haecceities will affirm that *a*=*a*. So it seems wrong to equate having an haecceity with claiming an object is identical with itself.

Second, B says that when one specifies a property had by an object *a*, one expects to be told "something" about *a*. But B is "left waiting" when the property in question is *being identical with a*. One immediate question raised by this objection is about the nature of being told "something" about an object. What precisely does that mean? Let's take "being told something" here to mean that we are told something *qualitative* about the object in question: That it's red, or round, or has wheels. As an empirical matter then, B surely is right. Usually when I ask about the properties something has, I expect to get qualitative answers. But this psychological fact doesn't tell us whether there's something wrong with the claim that object *a* differs from object *b* in that object *a* exemplifies *being identical with a* and *b* doesn't. Indeed, that B is left waiting seems B's fault. In a discussion of the identity of indiscernibles (especially in the 20th century), to expect only qualitative properties to be discussed is to have unreasonable expectations.

But isn't there something to Interlocutor B's objection that a property like *being identical with Socrates* is trivial? Perhaps. Consider another property that Socrates exemplifies, *being snubnosed*. If I am told that Socrates exemplifies the latter, I learn something about Socrates—that he's snubnosed. If I am told that Socrates exemplifies *being identical with Socrates*, I'm not told anything new about Socrates.[19] So far all this seems right. But there's nothing in this that suggests there is something *wrong* with the less-informative haecceity. Perhaps, then, there is something of the trivial about *being Socrates*. But it's not obviously objectionably trivial, and we should expect further argument to show that it is trivial in a problematic way.

3.2.2   Haecceities are Like Bare Particulars

A second objection to haecceities is that haecceities are like bare particulars or bare substratum, and bare particulars and bare substratum are objectionable.[20] We find this objection in E.J. Lowe:

> How might we refer to such a putative particular property, say of material sphere *A*? Presumably, we might refer to one such property, if nowise else, as *A*'s particular property of being identical with *A*. But how would this entity differ from *A*'s substratum [bare particular], assuming that is to exist, too (Lowe [87], p. 88)?

Lowe is not the first to associate haecceities with bare particulars. Some have likened Scotus' haecceities to bare particulars (see Park [98] for discussion). Perhaps, at first, one can see why one would link bare particulars and haecceities. Both are generally taken to be obscure entities that we have difficulty saying something positive (perhaps in multiple senses) about. Perhaps, then, they're the same thing? But I think we can see that they are very different sorts of things. A bare particular is a concrete entity in which qualities inhere. Locke claimed that the bare particular itself didn't have any properties. More recently, it has been suggested that the bare particular of, say, a book has bookish properties (Sider [123]). I have argued elsewhere that either suggestion is problematic and that the notion of a bare particular is based on a bad metaphysical picture (Davidson [45], p. 348; see also Section 2.2.1 of this book). Whatever one thinks of bare particulars, however, they're different animals from haecceities. An haecceity is either a hylomorphic or mereological part of a thing, or a property with the thing

66 Haecceity

as a constituent, or a primitive property. None of these things are like bare particulars.

Though it is true that sometimes the nature of haecceity is thought to be mysterious (though see Chapter 2 of this book!), there is no reason to identify them with bare particulars. Indeed, one may believe in haecceities and reject bare particulars, as I do. I do concede Lowe's conditional, though. If haecceities were bare particulars, that would be a problem for haecceities.

3.2.3 Chisholm's Property-Conceivability Objection

In his book *The First Person*, Roderick Chisholm argues that no property is such that it requires a concrete object to conceive of it.

> [W]e may say:
>
> (P2) Consider any property (other than the property of conceiving and what it entails): if the property is possibly such that nothing exemplifies it, then it is possibly such that (a) nothing exemplifies it and (b) something conceives it.
>
> This principle implies that no property is such that it can be conceived only by reference to a contingent thing (Chisholm [29], p. 7).

Why might this be thought to be a problem for haecceities? It would seem that I conceive the haecceity of my desk, say, only by reference to (or thinking of) a contingent thing—my desk.

I don't think this is a serious problem for haecceities. First, it's not clear why we should accept that a property can't only be conceived by reference to a contingent thing. We don't get an argument for it from Chisholm. It's not at all evidently true, and it seems like it is a principle that is made-to-order to do away with haecceities.

Second, is it true that every haecceity is conceived only by reference to a contingent thing? What about haecceities of necessary existents? Further, suppose constituentism about haecceities is true. Then perhaps if I grasp the haecceity of a contingent object, I make reference to a contingent thing. But if primitivism about haecceities is true, then why can't it be that each haecceity is possibly conceived without reference to a contingent thing? Maybe God conceives of every haecceity without reference to a contingent thing. Or maybe in some other world some other near-omniscient being conceives of every haecceity without reference to a contingent thing.

If we think that haecceities are contingent existents, then perhaps we can generate a particular case where an haecceity is possibly conceived only by reference to a contingent thing. It might be that there is an haecceity H in the actual world, α, where we are only able to conceive of H by reference to a

Haecceity 67

contingent thing. Suppose also that in α there are no other beings capable of conceiving of haecceities–no God, angels, or the like. It may be that though H exists in other worlds, it doesn't exist in any world where there is an individual capable of conceiving it without reference to a contingent thing.

But this returns us to our initial concern. Even if we suppose there are properties that are conceivable only by reference to a contingent thing, there's no reason to think that this fact spells trouble for the properties in question. Hence, I don't think that the believer in haecceities has anything to worry about from Chisholm's property conceivability objection.

3.2.4 The Further Feature Objection

According to this objection, there must be some feature that distinguishes an haecceity from any other haecceity. But we are not able to make sense of what that element is. Here are statements of a further feature objection from Michael Loux and Roderick Chisholm, respectively.

> Individual essences enable the ontologist to clarify the notion of a substance only if it is possible for him to identify in nontrivial terms the uniquely individuating component in which the individual essences...differ. But it is unclear that this is possible. What, for example, is it to exemplify the attribute of *being identical with Socrates*? Presumably, it is to be a living substance of a certain kind–a human being; but, of course, there has to be more here, some uniquely individuating feature in virtue of which *being identical with Socrates* is an attribute distinct from *being identical with Plato* and *being identical with Aristotle*. It is difficult, however, to see how we can identify this additional component except in the most blatantly circular terms–as the attribute of being identical with Socrates (Loux [85], p. 177).

> But if I can grasp my individual essence [haecceity], then I ought also to be able to single it out in those features that are unique to it. If *being identical with me* is my individual essence and *being identical with you* is yours, then, presumably, each analyses into personhood and something else as well—one something in my case and another in yours—but I haven't the faintest what this something else might be (Chisholm [29], p. 16).

In the last chapter, I argued that constituentism is the correct view of haecceity. What, then, could the constituentist say about the further feature objection? Consider first, Loux's statement of the view. Loux asks for the feature that makes *being identical with Socrates* a different attribute from *being identical with Plato*. The constituentist has a ready answer here: One has Socrates as a constituent and lacks Plato, and the other

68 *Haecceity*

has Plato as a constituent and lacks Socrates. We can see the constituentist also has a ready reply to Chisholm's statement of the further feature objection. The key difference between *being identical with me* (in the case of Chisholm) and *being identical with you* is that the former has Chisholm as a constituent and not you, and the latter has you as a constituent and not Chisholm. (I'm not sure why Chisholm thinks an haecceity analyzes into personhood.)

Do other views of haecceity have a reply to the further feature objection? The objection might seem to have the most bite against the primitivist. The primitivist about haecceity isn't able to point to a different element between *being Socrates* and *being Plato*. They just are distinct properties. This might not be a damning objection to primitivism, however. Arguably, everyone who believes in Platonic properties is a primitivist about most properties. What is the difference between the properties *being red* and *being a tree*? These properties don't have constituents that differ between them. They just are different properties. The primitivist simply says the same thing about haecceities. Thus, I don't think this objection is a *serious* problem for the primitivist. But it is a (weak) *prima facie* strength of constituentism over primitivism that the constituentist has a ready reply to the further feature objection.

The hylomorphic and non-hylomorphic partist will also be unable to point to elements that distinguish *being Plato* from *being Socrates*. For partists, haecceities are simple entities, and there's nothing further to be said about why this is Plato's haecceity rather than Socrates'.

3.2.5 The Common Feature Objection

The common feature objection to haecceities, like the further feature objection, considers elements present in distinct haecceities, like *being Socrates* and *being Plato*. The common feature objection, however, asks the believer in haecceities to explain what *being Socrates and being Plato* have in common (beyond exemplifying *being an haecceity*) that makes them both haecceities. (We saw elements of this objection in Chapter 2 in our discussion of strengths of constituentism over primitivism.) As with the further feature objection, the constituentist has a ready answer here. The slot-theoretic constituentist will say that each has as an element—the *is identical with* relation—along with an object that exemplifies the haecceity. The *sui generis* constituentist will say that each has as an element the *sui generis* abstract object *being identical with x*, along with an object that exemplifies the haecceity. As with the further feature objection, the partist and primitivist have no such account available and must deny there is any common feature between *being Socrates* and *being Plato* that explains why they are haecceities rather than any other sort of property. Also as with the further feature objection, I don't think this is a serious objection to non-constituentist views; however, that the constituentist has a reply to the common feature objection is a (perhaps weak) *prima facie* consideration in favor of constituentism.

3.2.6 The Wrong-Direction Objection

This is an objection to those like Adams and Rosenkrantz who think that individuation of particulars is by haecceity. According to the wrong-direction objection, individuation of haecceities should be by particulars, rather than the converse. E.J. Lowe gives this sort of objection in a review of Rosenkrantz's book:

> One is inclined to protest that if there is such a property as the property of *being identical with a*, then it is this property which is to be individuated in terms of a, the object which possesses it, rather than *vice versa*. Haecceitism [that particulars are individuated by haecceities] seems to put the cart before the horse in just the same way as someone would who proposed to individuate an object a in terms of its unit set, {a} (Lowe [86], p. 204).

We don't really get a fully-fledged argument from Lowe here; it's more of a statement of intuition. The intuition is that individuation of particulars is prior to individuation of haecceities and that if one individuates the other we should say that particulars individuate haecceities. This is an Ockhamist sort of intuition, the inclusion of haecceities notwithstanding. As we saw earlier in the chapter, it is very difficult to construct successful arguments against a view of individuation like Ockham's in favor of the necessity of haecceity for individuation. So, I think that Lowe is right here to push against arguments that one needs haecceity to individuate particulars. As we also saw in this chapter, however, there are semantic arguments for haecceity that are unaffected by the failure of individuative arguments for haecceity. So, even if Lowe is right about the direction of individuation, there still is a class of arguments available for establishing the existence of haecceities. Following Lowe on individuation doesn't by itself entail there are no haecceities.

3.2.7 The Haecceitistic Euthyphro Dilemma

Jason Bowers and Meg Wallace give what they call "a haecceitic Euthyphro problem" [20]. They call the view that necessarily everything has an haecceity, "Haecceitism."[21] Their "Euthyphro dilemma" arises when the Haecceitist gives an account of something's coming into existence. Suppose there is fission of an amoeba *A* into two amoebas *B* and *C*. When *B* and

C come into being, the Haecceitist will say that two haecceities are instantiated that weren't instantiated before: *being B* and *being C*. The dilemma from Bowers and Wallace then is this: (i) Are the haecceities *being B* and *being C* instantiated because two new entities come into being? Or (ii) do two new things come into being because *being B* and *being C* are instantiated?[22] Bowers and Wallace say the Haecceitist can't accept (i) because she is committed to haecceities individuating, rather than being individuated by, particulars. The Haecceitist can't accept (ii) because she can't give an account of how we get two haecceities from just the one before the split. Thus, Haecceitism is false.

It seems to me that Bowers and Wallace's arguments that the Haecceitist can't accept either horn of the dilemma are problematic. Start with the argument that the believer in haecceities can't accept (i) and that the two haecceities are instantiated because two new entities have come into being. The problem for the believer in haecceities is that this doesn't let the haecceities do the work of individuating the two new objects, and this is something that contradicts a core tenet of Haecceitism. However, as we've seen, one may believe in haecceities for semantic reasons and reject that they do work in individuating particulars. So, the Haecceitist may grasp the first horn of the dilemma.

Let us turn to the claim that the Haecceitist is unable to accept (ii), the second horn of the dilemma. Bowers and Wallace claim the Haecceitist cannot give an account of how we go from one haecceity before the split to two haecceities after the split. They entertain several possibilities, including that the original (abstract) haecceity (*being A*) splits; the original haecceity gives some of its "intensity" to the two new ones, the way a light source consisting of multiple light bulbs may give its intensity to two separate light sources made of subsets of the original bulbs; and that A is identical with A's haecceity and thus each splits in the case of fission. These three scenarios are rejected. They reject the first scenario because as abstract objects haecceities don't have parts and thus can't split. They reject the second as requiring an account of "dimming" and "intensity" and related concepts around the light bulb analogy. They reject the third because identifying an individual and its haecceity won't allow one to use haecceities to individuate particulars. Thus, the second horn of the dilemma isn't open to the Haecceitist either.

It seems to me that Bowers and Wallace are right to reject these three solutions. An abstract haecceity can't split, and something like intensity and dimming of haecceities don't make sense. I don't think that the identification of the individual with haecceity should be rejected on grounds of individuation, though; rather, an amoeba isn't identical with its haecceity because they are different sorts of objects. An amoeba is a concrete biological entity with vacuoles and a nucleus, and an haecceity is either an abstract property capable of being instantiated or is a simple part of a concrete object. What, then, should the Haecceitist who thinks that post-fission we have new objects because we have new haecceities say? How do we get the two new haecceities from the original single one? I think that this sort of Haecceitist should say that it is a primitive, ungrounded fact that we go from one haecceity to two haecceities when fission happens. The Haecceitist who accepts the second horn of the dilemma wants to individuate particulars with haecceities. Thus, this sort of Haecceitist pushes individuation of particulars up to the level of haecceity. What then explains how the haecceities line up with the particulars for this sort of theorist? This has to be a primitive sort of fact for this Haecceitist.

Thus, I contend that the Haecceitist can grasp either horn of Bowers and Wallace's dilemma. She may say that we have two new instantiated haecceities post-fission because we have two new objects post-fission. Or, she may say that we have two new objects post-fission because we have two new instantiated haecceities and that it is a primitive fact that we have two new instantiated haecceities post-fission. Thus, I don't think the believer in haecceities should think that there are serious problems for her view in the arguments we have from Bowers and Wallace.[23]

That said, the sort of Haecceitist one is may drive rejection of one horn or another. If I'm a constituentist, accepting the first horn and rejecting the second looks most plausible to me. If concrete objects are constituents of haecceities, then it seems best to let the new objects explain the new haecceities, rather than the other way round. The primitivist or partist presumably could reject either horn and accept the other.

In this chapter I've argued that there are good semantic arguments for the existence of haecceities and that the constituentist about haecceity has nothing to fear from the extant objections to haecceity. Thus, we have reason to think that there are haecceities. In the next chapter, we take up an issue often considered alongside the existence and nature of haecceities: the distinction between qualitative and quidditative properties.

Notes

1 See Bates [13], ch. 4 for discussion.
2 Or it may (also) be that post-Scotus (a few peripheral Scotists aside) haecceities were not seriously embraced again until after Leibniz, and post-Leibniz philosophers were primarily interested in questions of distinctness rather than singleness. (This is so in spite of the fact that Leibniz himself was concerned with questions both of singleness as well as distinctness.)
3 Adams [4] and Diekemper [49] call these arguments from spatial dispersal/dispersion (respectively).
4 Adams [4] and Diekemper [49] call these arguments from temporal dispersal/dispersion (respectively).

5 Adams considers arguments for haecceities in his recent book (Adams [8]), though his discussion of the arguments is more thorough in Adams [4]. Thus, I will draw from the earlier paper in this section of the book.
6 The formal structure of the globe argument carries over to the other four arguments Adams provides for the existence of haecceities. They differ only with respect to what the distinct objects in (3) are. As a result I will render only this first argument with numbered premises.
7 To put this more pithily, one might say that we have primitive identity without primitive thisness.
8 I think that Leibniz himself probably would agree with Adams' characterization that necessarily every object o exemplifies the property *being identical with* o (where the claim is properly translated to take into account Leibniz's nominalism–which I will ignore in this section). For Leibniz, such a property is a maximal conjunction of qualitative properties. Each conjunction is necessarily had by only one object.
9 See papers in Ludlow and Martin [88] for discussion.
10 See endnote 1 in the Introduction for more on haecceitism.
11 That is, that if x and y have all the same qualitative properties, then $x = y$.
12 For our purposes, we'll assume that Adams in this conversation doesn't reject outright as impossible bilocated objects.
13 As seems to be the case from discussion in the literature.
14 One might wonder (as a reviewer did) how these sorts of semantic arguments differ from the "easy" ontological entailments of philosophers like Amie Thomasson [132] or Stephen Schiffer [122]. According to Thomasson and Schiffer (and others), there is an analytic entailment between the truth of claims like "the table is brown" and the existence of a property *being brown*. I deny that this entailment is analytic. I simply don't believe that competent speakers of English wouldn't have noticed such entailments before the 21st century. We may make the same point in the context of semantic arguments for haecceity. If there is an entailment between the fact that that "is identical with Socrates" is meaningful; and the existence of *being Socrates*, the entailment is not analytic. The existence of haecceity is not to be had that easily. Thus, I regard this "easy" metametaphysical approach in a manner not entirely differently from that in which I regard logical positivism. Both the easy ontologists and the positivists thought that the effort of philosophers for millennia was wasted and could have been avoided if they had merely reflected on the plain meanings (or lack thereof) of the terms they were using. How could this be? Wouldn't competent users of English (or German, Greek, or Latin) have noticed this earlier?
15 Frege seems to have thought that the idea of a proposition with a concrete entity as a constituent was bizarre. See his exchange with Russell (Davidson [42], p. 53).
16 Questions of opacity seem most salient with names, though opacity may also arise with indexicals.
17 I explore different conceptions of actualism and defend this one in my [47], ch. 1.
18 My reasoning here follows Plantinga's ([105], p. 120).
19 Or at least nothing new if I already believed in haecceities.

20 Here bare particulars or bare substratum are the sorts of things that Locke or Gustav Bergmann believed in–some entity that, while itself lacking properties or qualities, supports the exemplification of properties or qualities by an object. See Section 2.2.1 for discussion.
21 Bowers and Wallace don't capitalize the word when giving the name of the view. However, I will capitalize "Haecceitism" and cognates in this context, as the name "haecceitism" is usually used for a supervenience claim that is conceptually independent of the existence of haecceities. See the Introduction for more about haecceitism (the supervenience claim).
22 At least conceptually there is room for rejecting the premise that neither the new objects explain the new haecceities or conversely. (Thanks to Jim Van Cleve for the objection.) Then, the existence of the new objects is entirely independent of the existence of the new haecceities. I think the reason to insist that the new haecceities depend on the new objects or conversely is that for any believer in haecceities there is a close tie between haecceity and object that exemplifies the haecceity such that their existence couldn't be totally independent of each other.
23 Skiles [124] offers a critique of Bowers and Wilkins employing contemporary grounding theory. I am skeptical about contemporary grounding theory for the sorts of reasons one finds in Daly ([37] and [38] and Hofweber ([67]).

4 Qualitative and Quidditative Properties

We find in the recent metaphysical literature a distinction between two sorts of properties. This distinction has several names: the qualitative/non-qualitative property distinction, the pure/impure property distinction, the haecceitistic/non-haecceitistic property distinction, and the qualitative/quidditative property distinction. Here I will adopt the qualitative/quidditative terminology. In this chapter, I want to set out and defend a novel account of the qualitative/quidditative distinction. This account, which I will call "quidditative constituentism," may be seen as a conceptual extension of the constituentism about haecceity that I defend in this book. I will argue here that quidditative constituentism is superior to other extant accounts of the qualitative/quidditative distinction.

4.1 The Qualitative/Quidditative Distinction Intuitively Characterized

In a number of places, we see the qualitative/quidditative distinction mentioned in a way designed to provide a rough-and-ready understanding of the distinction, though it is not further examined. For instance, we see in Alvin Plantinga's "On Existentialism" the following statement:

> Let us say that a property is *quidditative* if it is either a thisness [haecceity] or involves a thisness in a certain way. We could try to spell out the way in question in formal and recursive details; but instead let me just give some examples. *Being identical with Nero* or *being Nero* is a quidditative property; but so are *being more blood-thirsty than Nero, being either Nero or Cicero, being either Nero or wise, being possibly wiser than Nero, being believed by Nero to be treacherous,* and *being such that there is someone more bloodthirsty than Nero.* We may contrast the notion of a quidditative property with that of a *qualitative* property. Again, I shall not try to give a *definition* of this notion; but examples would be *being wise, being 14 years*

DOI: 10.4324/9781003439738-5

old, being angry, being learned, being six feet from a desk, and the like (Plantinga [109], p. 158).

We also see a nod in the direction of the distinction without further pursual in John Hawthorne's "Identity" entry in *The Oxford Handbook of Metaphysics*.

> "One might wonder whether if x and y share every 'non-haecceitistic property' then x and y are identical (where haecceitistic properties–such as *being identical to John* or *being the daughter of Jim*–are those which, in some intuitive way, make direct reference to a particular individual(s))" (Hawthorne [64], p. 107).

We have from Plantinga and Hawthorne some idea of what quidditative properties are. For Plantinga, they involve haecceities, and for Hawthorne, they are directly about an individual.[1] For most purposes, this sort of rough-and-ready characterization is sufficient. It would be better for our purposes in this book, however, if we were able to give an analysis of the qualitative/quidditative distinction. We will try to do this in this chapter. We begin by first considering the merits of a number of different extant analyses of the distinction.

4.2 The Linguistic View

The proponent of the linguistic view about the qualitative/quidditative distinction grounds the distinction in the language used to express each sort of property. Robert Adams in "Primitive Thisness and Primitive Identity" states a view like this:

> We might try to capture the idea by saying that a property is purely qualitative–a suchness–if and only if it could be expressed, in a language sufficiently rich, without the aid of such referential devices as proper names, proper adjectives and verbs (such as "Leibnizian" and "pegasizes"), indexical expressions, and referential uses of definite descriptions (Adams [4], p. 7).

We also get a statement of the linguistic view from Gary Rosenkrantz:

> The difference between the pure and the impure is often explained in linguistic terms. An impure property is described as one which is expressed by a predicate manufactured with the help of a proper name or indexical term designating a concrete object; a pure property is characterized as one which is expressed by a predicate which is free from any such singular term (Rosenkrantz [116], p. 516).

On the linguistic view about the qualitative/quidditative distinction, a property is quidditative because it is expressed by a predicate or gerundial phrase with rigid terms in it. A qualitative property is a property that is expressed by a predicate or gerundial phrase with no rigid terms in it.

I think we can see, however, that the linguistic view isn't a plausible account of the qualitative/quidditative distinction. The main problem with the linguistic view about the qualitative/quidditative distinction is that it gets the order of explanation between quidditative/qualitative properties and language use the wrong way round. The linguistic view grounds the qualitative/quidditative distinction in features of language rather than features of the properties themselves. Surely, the reason why we express quidditative properties with predicates with rigid terms is because the properties are "already" quidditative independently of language use. Our language use doesn't make them quidditative or qualitative. Thus, we should reject the linguistic view about the qualitative/quidditative distinction. Let us then turn to a second analysis of the distinction.

4.3   The Entailment View

A second analysis of the qualitative/quidditative property distinction grounds the distinction in the existence entailment of a particular object. We will call this second position *the entailment view*. The proponent of the entailment view about the qualitative/quidditative distinction holds that a quidditative property is a property whose instantiation entails the existence of a particular object, and a qualitative property is a property that doesn't. We see this analysis from a number of different philosophers. Katherine Hawley is a proponent of this view:

> "Qualitative" more usually picks out those properties and relations whose instantiation does not require the existence of any specific object: this *composing something* usually counts as qualitative, while *composing the Eiffel Tower* is non-qualitative (Hawley [63], p. 102).

Gary Rosenkrantz also defends an entailment view about the qualitative/quidditative distinction. For Rosenkrantz, a quidditative property is a property the instantiation of which entails the existence of a particular concrete object (Rosenkrantz [116]).

At first, the entailment view appears promising. It correctly classes *being red* as qualitative, as its instantiation doesn't entail the existence of any particular object. It also gets correct that *being Socrates* is quidditative, as its instantiation does entail the existence of a particular object, namely, Socrates. However, the entailment view about the qualitative/quidditative distinction runs into trouble with certain types of negative quidditative

Qualitative and Quidditative Properties 77

properties.[2] Consider a world W in which I don't exist. Individuals in W (say, the number three) have the property *being distinct from me*. If the exemplification of *being distinct from me* entails the existence of anything, it is me. Yet, it is exemplified in W and I don't exist in W.

Thus, the defender of the entailment view will need to ease the sting of the claim that no one in W exemplifies the property *being distinct from me*. The most natural way to do this is to adopt a property version of the inside/outside truth distinction. Then, one might say *being distinct from me* is exemplified outside W, though not inside W. This would mirror the claim that *I do not exist* is true outside W, though not inside W. There have been various attempts to analyze inside and outside truth. I argue in Chapter 5 of this book that no extant reductive analysis of inside and outside truth works and that there is reason to think that there is no such analysis to be had. I suspect the same goes for exemplification inside and outside a world—that is, there is no analysis of the distinction to be had. But if one already is committed to a distinction between truth inside and truth outside a world, one may be tempted by the same sort of distinction at the level of property exemplification as a way of dealing with problems of negative quidditative properties.

Even if one does adopt a property view of the inside/outside truth distinction to deal with negative quidditative properties, there is another problem with the entailment view. (A similar problem will arise with the relational view that we will examine later in the chapter.) The entailment view grounds a property's being quidditative in the fact that its instantiation entails the existence of another object. However, that a property is quidditative should rest in features of the property itself. Even if we were to grant that the instantiation of a quidditative property entails the existence of a particular object, that fact itself can't be what explains why it is quidditative. Rather, that it is quidditative should come from the property itself, and features of the property itself would then imply that its instantiation entails there is the additional object.

We turn to two analyses that are similar in spirit to the entailment view—the dependence view and the relational view.

4.4 The Dependence View

David Ingram [71] sets out an account of the qualitative/quidditative distinction that resembles the entailment view from the last section. On Ingram's view, however, the *existence* of a quidditative property depends on the existence of some other object. We will call his view *the dependence view*.

For Ingram, quidditative properties "involve" other entities. He defines involvement as follows:

> A [quidditative] property N involves some entity x insofar as N depends on x in a specific way, that is, N non-rigidly ontologically depends on x (Ingram [71], pp. 58-59).

Non-rigid ontological dependence of A on B occurs where B must exist in order for A to exist initially, though A may later exist without B (Ingram [71], pp. 66–67). Then, for Ingram a quidditative property is a property that requires another entity to exist in order for it to exist, at least at first. All other properties are qualitative properties.

I think we can see that the dependence view falls short as an account of the qualitative/quidditative distinction. First, this account entails that haecceities and other quidditative properties of contingent existences are themselves contingent existences. Our *account* of the qualitative/quidditative distinction shouldn't by itself foreclose on the possibility that there are necessarily existing haecceities and other similar quidditative properties of contingent existences. That is, our analysis of the qualitative/quidditative distinction shouldn't settle the debate between Alvin Plantinga and Robert Adams about the nature of haecceities. This is true even if we go on to decide that Robert Adams is right in thinking that haecceities and other related quidditative properties of contingent existences are themselves contingent existences.

Second, like the entailment view, negative quidditative properties pose a concern for the dependence view. Consider again a world W in which I don't exist. Entities in W exemplify *being distinct from me*. Thus, we should say that *being distinct from me* exists in W. If *being distinct from me* depended on anything for its existence, however, it would depend on me. Yet, I don't exist in W. This suggests that *being distinct from me* doesn't depend on anything for its existence.[3]

Third, the dependence view should be fleshed out to explain why it is that a quidditative property depends for its existence on another object. What is it about each quidditative property such that its existence depends on existence of some other object? The only way to do this that I can see would be to construe quidditative properties as having constituents, as we will consider below in Section 4.6. But if one thinks that quidditative properties are those with constituents, why not locate their quidditative nature in having constituents rather than in depending for their existence on other objects?

4.5 The Relational View

A fourth view about the nature of the qualitative/quidditative distinction is *the relational view*. According to the relational view, that a property is quidditative is grounded in the fact that necessarily anything that instantiates it stands in a relation to a particular object. The relational view is a widely held view as to the nature of the qualitative/quidditative distinction.

Michael Loux is a defender of the relational view. In *Substance and Attribute*, he writes:

> I have so far explained the distinction [between pure and impure properties] in metaphorical terms, speaking of properties of "incorporating" or not "incorporating" substances. We can explain the distinction more precisely if we say that a property, P, is impure just in case there is some relation R, and some substance, s, such that necessarily, for any object x, x exemplifies P if and only if x enters into R with s and that a property P is pure just in case P is not impure. We can see how this account of the distinction operates if we consider the properties I have used as examples. Corresponding to the property, *being married to Henry VIII*, there is the relation, *being married to*, and the substance, Henry VIII; and it is necessarily true that an object exemplifies *being married to Henry VIII* if and only if she bears that relation to that substance; consequently *being married to Henry VIII* is an impure property (Loux [85], p. 133).

Suppose then that x exemplifies *being taller than Socrates*. Necessarily x exemplifies this if and only if x stands in the *being taller than* relation to Socrates. Or suppose x exemplifies *being identical with Socrates*. Necessarily x exemplifies this if and only if x stands in the *is identical with* relation to Socrates. And so on.

There are several problems with Loux's relational view of the qualitative/quantitative distinction. The first is a problem of the sort that we saw with the entailment view in Section 4.3. A quidditative property on Loux's account is a property P the instantiation of which by x entails and is entailed by x's standing in some relation R to some object y. But whether P is quidditative should have to do with features of P, not with whether its exemplification by x entails that x stands in a relation to an object. We should want to know what it is about P *itself* that makes it quidditative.

Loux's account suffers from a second problem. Suppose that classical theism is true: that God exists necessarily and is essentially omniscient. Consider any individual x and property P. Necessarily x exemplifies P just if x stands in the *is believed to instantiate P by* relation to God. Then, on

80 *Qualitative and Quidditative Properties*

Loux's account a classical theist would have to say that every property is quidditative.[4]

There is another problem that Loux's relational account encounters. Consider a qualitative property necessarily had by everything, like *being self-identical*.[5] On Loux's analysis, this property would be quidditative. Necessarily, any x (say, me) exemplifies *being self-identical* just if x stands in the *existing in the same world as* relation with the number three.

Thus, we can see that Loux's relational account doesn't correctly sort qualitative and quidditative properties. Given these sorts of problems, a natural way to try to fix a relational account is to try to limit the class of relations specified in our definition of the distinction. Edward J. Khamara tries to do exactly this. He gives the following definition of an impure property.

> A property, P, is impure if and only if there is at least one individual, y, such that, for any individual, x, x's having P consists in x's having a certain relation to y (Khamara [77], p. 145).

On Khamara's definition, x's having the quidditative property P *consists in* x's standing in a relation R to y. It is not enough that x stand in R to y. This looks like progress, as we can limit the scope of relations in the sort of way we saw we needed to do with Loux's analysis.

I have concerns about Khamara's analysis, however. First, we're owed an account of "consists in." It will need to be spelled out in a way that doesn't straight-out entail that P is quidditative. We seek an informative analysis of the qualitative/quidditative distinction, not one that builds the distinction into the analysis. Giving such a non-circular account of "consists in" may be doable, but Khamara doesn't do it, and I'm not certain how it could be done. Until we have an analysis of "consists" in, we should not think of Khamara's attempt as a successful reductive analysis of the qualitative/quidditative distinction.

Second, as with the entailment view, Khamara's analysis tries to ground a property P's being quidditative in *something else* besides features of P. Quidditative properties should be quidditative in virtue of features they themselves have, not in virtue of relations the things that exemplify them stand in to other objects. Thus, there is a second reason why I don't think that Khamara's version of the relational view will work.

Vera Hoffmann-Kolss [66] also gives a relational analysis of the quidditative/qualitative distinction. Her final analysis is as follows:

> (RC)₃ (a) A property P is basic qualitative iff [...] it is not the case that there is a two-place relation R such that:
>
>> (i) There is a possible individual a, such that for all possible x, x's having P is logically equivalent to x's standing in R to a.

(ii) It is logically possible that there is an individual having the existential derivative of R but not P.

(b) P is basic haecceitistic if neither P nor ~P is basic qualitative.

(c) P is haecceitistic if P is either basic haecceitistic or can be recursively generated out of haecceitistic properties according to the rules of modal predicate logic (Hoffmann-Kolss [66], p. 1007).

Her analysis is complex. For our purposes here, we may note that a property P is quidditative and is grounded principally in the logical equivalence of an object x's having P and x's standing in a relation R to some other object a.

Because of how we are to understand logical equivalence in Hoffmann-Kolss's analysis,[6] this relational account may allow one to avoid two of the problems we saw with Loux's relational account. Consider first the objection to Loux's account. According to it, the classical theist has to say that every property is quidditative. Hoffmann-Kolss wants logical possibility to be broader than metaphysical possibility; thus, a proposition p and a proposition q may be metaphysically equivalent without being logically equivalent. Loux's account had trouble with the fact that (necessarily) for any x, x has a property P if and only if x stands in the *is believed to instantiate P by* relation to God. Hoffmann-Kolss may say that there are logically (though not metaphysically) possible worlds where x can have P even x doesn't stand in the *is believed to instantiate P by* relation to God. Such a world might be one where x exists and God doesn't. Or, it might be a world where God exists but isn't omniscient. Regardless, though, in some of the relevant worlds x has P without x standing in the *is believed to instantiate P by* relation to God.

There is a analogous reply that Hoffmann-Kolss might make to the second problem that Loux's relational view has with sorting qualitative and quidditative properties. The second objection to Loux's account is that on it one is committed to saying that a property like *being self-identical* is quidditative. This commitment comes from the fact that it is true that necessarily for any x, x exemplifies *being self-identical* if and only if x stands in the *existing in the same world as* relation to the number three. By way of reply, Hoffmann-Kolss might say there are logically (though not metaphysically) possible worlds where the number three doesn't exist. In one of those worlds I exist. Then, it is false that I exemplify *being self-identical* if and only if I stand in the *existing in the same world as* relation to the number three. This biconditional doesn't hold so long as we understand it to involve logical rather than metaphysical necessity. We may see then that hyperintensionality in Hoffmann-Kolss's analysis is designed to avoid the sorts of counterexamples that affected an analysis like that of Loux.

Does Hoffmann-Kolss have a successful reply to these two objections to a relational account like Loux's? It's not at all obvious to me that we can make sense of necessity broader than metaphysical or broad logical necessity.[7] It's even less clear to me that we can make sense of its being logically possible that a necessarily existing object not exist. Do we want to say that number three cannot not exist (full stop) and say that it might not exist? Do we want to say that God cannot not exist (full stop) *and* that God could not exist, and in such a case *x* could exemplify *P*? Suppose we think that necessarily everything depends on God in some strong sense, even necessarily existing abstracta.[8] In such a case, could *x* still exemplify *P* if God didn't exist?

Thus, I have concerns about the type of hyperintensionality Hoffmann-Kolss employs in her relational account of the qualitative/quidditative distinction. Suppose, though, that we're fine with these sort of claims about logically possible though metaphysically impossible worlds. A new concern then arises for an account like that of Hoffman-Kolss: In that, it will be hard not to class all properties as qualitative properties. Consider *being taller than Socrates*. It is quidditative crucially because if *x* instantiates *being taller than Socrates*, *x* stands in the *being taller than* relation to Socrates. But aren't there logically possible (though metaphysically impossible) worlds where this doesn't hold? Does it violate the laws of logic that *x* exemplify *being taller than Socrates* and not stand in the *being taller than* relation to Socrates? Maybe it does. But it's not obvious it does.[9] The relational theorist appealing to this sort of hyperintensionality will have to take care that, in trying to respond to worries of there being too many quidditative properties on a relational account, there aren't as a result too few.

Overall, then, it is not clear that appealing to logically possible though metaphysically impossible worlds as a way of invoking hyperintensionality will allow the relational theorist avoid these two problems that affect Loux's account. However, even if we suppose there is a reply to these problems in this sort of hyperintensionality, there remains a problem for Hoffman-Kolss's relational analysis. This is a problem that Loux's relational account also faced. The problem is that *P* is quidditative should be grounded in something about *P* itself, rather than relations that something that exemplifies *P* stands in to other objects. It may be that (necessarily) *x* exemplifies *P* if and only if *x* stands in *R* to some distinct object *a*. But this relational entailment itself needs an explanation. What is it about the property *P* such that this relational entailment holds?

We can see then that the entailment view and the extant varieties of the relational view of the qualitative/quidditative distinction appeal to something beyond the property in question *P* to explain that *P* is quidditative. We should insist on something about *P* itself that will explain why *P* is quidditative. We turn to an account that does exactly this.

4.6 Quidditative Constituentism

Quidditative constituentism about the qualitative/quidditative distinction is the view that a property *P*'s being quidditative is grounded in *P*'s having another object as a constituent. For instance, the properties *being Socrates* and *being taller than Socrates* are quidditative because each has Socrates as a constituent. For non-conjunctive or non-disjunctive properties, a property *P*'s having as a constituent some distinct object is necessary and sufficient for *P*'s being quidditative. For conjunctive or disjunctive properties, a property is quidditative when at least one of the conjuncts or disjuncts of the property has as a constituent some distinct object. So, *being red or being taller than Socrates* is quidditative because one disjunct of the property has Socrates as a constituent.

Quidditative constituentism is a view that may seem quite natural if one is already inclined to direct reference semantics. The direct reference theorist typically will draw a distinction between two sorts of propositions. The first is a purely qualitative proposition which is made up of properties and relations and contains no constituents that are referents of terms in a sentence which expresses the proposition. The second is a quidditative, singular proposition which does have as a constituent an object which is the referent of a term in a sentence which expresses the proposition. Thus, the direct reference theorist would distinguish between a singular proposition like *Socrates is snub-nosed* which has Socrates as a constituent, and a qualitative proposition like *The philosopher is snub-nosed*, which lacks Socrates or any other philosopher as a constituent. The quidditative constituentist marks a difference between qualitative and quidditative properties in an analogous way. Quidditative propositions and quidditative properties are of a piece. I take this to be a strength of the view.

One might think of quidditative constituentism as a special instance of the relational view. On quidditative constituentism, a property is quidditative if it stands in the *having as a constituent* relation to some distinct object—intuitively the object that exemplifies the quidditative property. The relation in question is a special one, for it is one that makes the distinct object *part* of the quidditative property. That the relation holds tells us something about the nature of the property itself. This was lacking in the other relational views we've examined.

Doesn't quidditative constituentism run into trouble with negative quidditative properties? Here's an argument it does. In a world W where I don't exist, the number three exemplifies the property *being distinct from me*. Thus, the property *being distinct from me* must exist in W. But it can't exist in W, as I'm not around to be a constituent of *being distinct from me*.

84 Qualitative and Quidditative Properties

There are three sorts of solutions to this problem. My preferred solution is to adopt independence actualism, the view on which an object may exemplify properties and stand in relations even though the object in question doesn't exist.[10] The independence actualist may say that *being distinct from me* may have me as a constituent in W, in spite of the fact that I don't exist in W. In particular, I may stand in the *being a constituent of* relation to *being distinct from me* even in a world like W where I don't exist.

A second solution to the these sorts of problems with negative quidditative properties is to adopt a property version of the inside/outside truth distinction. Earlier, we considered this as a strategy the entailment and dependence views might adopt as a reply to the argument from negative quidditative properties. I have reservations (which I explore in Section 5.1.4) about such a move at the level of inside/outside truth of propositions, and I suspect problems for that strategy will carry over to its analog in the case of proper exemplification.

A third solution is to adopt Meinongianism. For the Meinongian, I can be part of *being distinct from me* in W in spite of the fact that I don't exist in W. I am a nonexistent object in W, and nonexistent objects may stand in relations like *being a constituent of*.

I think then that there are various replies available to the quidditative constituentist about distinctness with non-actual individuals. I contend then that quidditative constituentism ought to be considered a serious contender as an account of the distinction between qualitative and quidditative properties. It offers a compelling account of the qualitative/quidditative property distinction that avoids problems that affect other analyses.

At several points in this book, we have encountered the question of whether there can be unexemplified haecceities. We turn to extended discussion of that issue in the next chapter.

Notes

1 I'm going to avoid Hawthorne's language of properties referring, as referring is the sort of thing that linguistic items or people do.
2 See Cowling [34] for further discussion.
3 Here, as with the entailment view, the dependence theorist may avail herself of the property exemplification version of truth inside/outside a world. See Section 5.1.4 for discussion of truth inside vs. outside a world.
4 Compare Khamara ([77], p. 146) for a similar sort of objection.
5 Note that this is different from the haecceity *being identical with myself*. The latter is quidditative and had necessarily only by me. *Being self-identical* necessarily is had by everything.
6 Thanks to Vera Hoffmann-Kolss for discussion of this issue.

7 See Plantinga [101] for discussion of broadly logical possibility and other modalities. See Jackson [72] and Chalmers [24] for further discussion of different types of modality.
8 See my [40], ch. 8 for discussion.
9 Uncertainty as to how to class this sort of case may push in the direction of not accepting logical possibilities that aren't metaphysical possibilities.
10 See Davidson [47] for an explication and defense of independence actualism.

5 Haecceity and Existence

Thus far in this book, we have taken haecceities to be properties. In this chapter, we will take up the question of whether haecceities, *qua* properties, depend for their existence on the entities that instantiate them. The question we seek to answer then is this: Can there be unexemplified haecceities? In the first part of the chapter, we will consider arguments for the possibility of unexemplified haecceities. In the second part of the chapter, we will consider arguments against the possibility of unexemplified haecceities. We will see that we have reason to think that there are unexemplified haecceities and that none of the arguments against the possibility of unexemplified haecceities are successful. Thus, I will argue we have a *prima facie* case for believing it is possible there be unexemplified haecceities.[1]

5.1 Arguments that Haecceities Don't Depend for Their Existence on the Objects that Instantiate Them

5.1.1 An Argument from an Actualist Modal Semantics

The first argument for the possibility of there being unexemplified haecceities comes from their use in providing actualist truth conditions for modal discourse. In Chapter 3, we discussed Alvin Plantinga's use of haecceities in giving actualist truth conditions for modal sentences. Here, we focus on the role of unexemplified haecceities in Plantinga's semantics. For Plantinga, haecceities are necessary existents. Thus, my haecceity exists in every world, whether or not I exist in a particular world. In Section 3.1.2, we considered the sentence

(S1) There could have been an object that doesn't actually exist.

(S1) is true in the actual world, α. Plantinga gives the following as truth conditions for (S1)'s truth in α: There exists an haecceity H that is not instantiated in α, but is instantiated in a world W that is distinct from α. Then, we can see that we are committed to unexemplified haecceities for Plantinga; H is such an haecceity.

The question then becomes whether we *need* unexemplified haecceities to give actualist truth conditions for modal sentences. Christopher Menzel [93] has argued that we don't; we may locate actualist truth conditions in primitive properties of models. I myself have argued that one can give actualist truth conditions by allowing objects to exemplify properties and stand in relations even though they do not exist (Davidson [47], ch. 3). By adopting this strategy—independence actualism—we may allow that an object o may exemplify properties and stand in relations at worlds where o doesn't exist. Suppose o doesn't exist at α, but does exist in a world distinct from α, W. Then, o may exemplify at α the properties *nonexistence* and *possibly existing*. That o has these properties at α entails the truth of (S1) at α. The independence actualist has no need of unexemplified haecceities in giving actualist truth conditions for sentences like (S1). Suppose, though, that Alan McMichael ([92], p. 62) is right in thinking that these sorts of alternate actualist semantics won't work. Then, the argument from actualist modal semantics will provide a convincing reason for thinking there are unexemplified haecceities for those who are actualists.

5.1.2 *The Argument from Negative Quidditative Properties*

A second argument that there can be unexemplified haecceities comes from tying them to certain negative quidditative properties. Consider the property *being distinct from Socrates*. Consider a world W1 where Socrates doesn't exist. Objects in W1 (say, the number three) exemplify *being distinct from Socrates*. Then, *being distinct from Socrates* exists in W1. But if *being distinct from Socrates* exists in W1, so does *being Socrates*. Thus, there can be unexemplified haecceities.

(A parallel argument will yield that there are unexemplified haecceities in the actual world, α. Consider the case of Sib, a sibling I would have had if a particular blastocyst had developed into a person.[2] In α, I exemplify *being distinct from Sib*. Thus, *being distinct from Sib* exists in α. However, if *being distinct from Sib* exists in α, so does *being Sib*. So, there actually are unexemplified haecceities.)

The argument from negative quidditative properties has three key premises. The first is that an object o in W1 exemplifies *being distinct from Socrates*. The second is that if a property P is exemplified in a world W, then P exists in W. The third is that if the property *being distinct from Socrates* exists in a world W1, then *being Socrates* exists in W1.

The first premise will look promising if one believes in abundant properties and isn't an existentialist in Plantinga's [109] sense of the term. One of the things that is true of o in W1 is that o is distinct from Socrates. Thus, o exemplifies the property *being distinct from Socrates*. If one is an existentialist, however, one will reject this first premise. Thus, it's not clear to me that we should think of the argument from negative quidditative properties as serving as an independent sort of argument for the possibility of unexemplified haecceities. But for the person who, like me, isn't antecedently a committed existentialist, the first premise will look plausible.

The second premise follows from serious actualism. It also will follow from any sort of independence actualism which requires properties to exist at a world *W1* to be exemplified at *W1*. (Embracing the view that some objects that don't exist may nevertheless exemplify properties and stand in relations doesn't commit one to thinking that such an object can exemplify any property or stand in any relation.)

The third premise in the argument from negative quidditative properties looks to be true. As we will see in Section 5.1.4, the arguments that tell against the existence of an unexemplified *being Socrates* tell against the existence of *being distinct from Socrates* in worlds where Socrates doesn't exist.

Thus, the argument from negative quidditative properties for unexemplified haecceities is unlikely to convince someone who antecedently denies that there are unexemplified haecceities. Such a person will simply deny that an object *o* in a world *W1* where Socrates doesn't exist exemplifies *being distinct from Socrates*. But from it we can see how one may move from negative quidditative properties being instantiated in a world to unexemplified haecceities existing there.

5.1.3 A Semantic Argument for Unexemplified Haecceities

Our third argument that there can be unexemplified haecceities is an extension of the semantic argument for the existence of haecceities involving predicates that we saw in Section 3.1.2. There we argued that haecceities serve as the semantic contents of predicates like "is Socrates." In this context, we can consider quidditative predicates where the object that would satisfy them doesn't exist. In a world *W* where Socrates doesn't exist, "is Socrates" is meaningful. The semantic content of "is Socrates" in *W* is the haecceity *being Socrates*. Thus, *being Socrates* exists in *W*.

(As with the argument from negative quidditative properties, we may run the same sort of argument in the actual world, α. In α, "is Sib" is meaningful. The semantic content of a predicate like "is Sib" is the haecceity *being Sib*. Thus, there exists actually the haecceity *being Sib*.)

There are places to resist this argument; they are the same places at which one may resist the argument in Section 3.1.2. One might object to the claim that propositions have constituents, as Trenton Merricks does [52], or that their constituents are the semantic values of the parts of the sentences that express them. One might also object to the claim that the semantic contents of predicates are properties or to the claim that haecceities are the only candidates for properties that quidditative predicates express. Or, one might object to the claim that only existing properties may serve as semantic contents of linguistic items.

But this argument looks compelling to me in the same way the argument in Section 3.1.2 looked compelling to me. The argument in each section is functionally the same; the difference is only in the class of predicates we're considering. Here, we extend that semantic argument to a different class of predicates. When we do so, we establish the existence of unexemplified haecceities.

5.1.4 A Modified Plantingan Argument

In "On Existentialism" [109], Alvin Plantinga gives an argument that singular propositions may exist even when the object they are about doesn't exist. We may modify his argument there to yield the conclusion that haecceities may exist even when the object that would exemplify them doesn't exist. The modified argument proceeds as follows:

1. It is possible Socrates doesn't exist.
2. Necessarily, if it is possible Socrates doesn't exist, then the proposition *Socrates does not exist* is possibly true.
3. Therefore, *Socrates does not exist* is possibly true.
4. Necessarily, if *Socrates does not exist* is true, *Socrates does not exist* exists.
5. Necessarily, if *Socrates does not exist* exists, *being Socrates* exists.
6. Therefore, it is possible that Socrates not exist and *being Socrates* exists.

What should we make of this argument? Someone like Williamson [141] or Linsky/Zalta [83] will reject (1). For them, Socrates exists in every world, as does everything else. This position has come to be known as *necessitism*. What do we do with the intuition that Socrates could have failed to exist? They deny this, but proffer the claim that Socrates is contingently concrete. At a world W where one would be tempted to say that Socrates doesn't exist, we instead say that Socrates is not concrete at W. For the necessitist, *being possibly non-concrete* is a proxy for *existing contingently*.

But surely (1) is true and Socrates is a contingent entity. If we are going to reject this modified Plantingan argument, we should do so on firmer grounds than that of accepting necessitism. Let us then grant the truth of (1). (We can note that if we could show that there could be unexemplified haecceities if some things don't exist necessarily, we still would have shown a substantial metaphysical claim.)

When considering a proposition like (2), the distinction between two sorts of truth with respect to a world often is invoked (see e.g. Prior

[113], Adams [5], Fine [52], Pollock [111, 112], Menzel [94], and Stalnaker [128, 129]).

Here is Kit Fine invoking this sort of distinction:

> One should distinguish between two notions of truth for propositions, the inner and the outer. According to the outer notion, a proposition is true in a possible world regardless of whether it exists in that world; according to the inner notion, a proposition is true in a possible world only if it exists in that world. We may put the distinction in terms of perspective. According to the outer notion, we can stand outside a world and compare the proposition with what goes on in the world in order to ascertain whether it is true. But according to the inner notion, we must first enter with the proposition into the world before entertaining its truth (Fine [52], p. 163).

Robert Adams uses similar language:

> A [possible world] that includes no singular proposition about me constitutes and describes a possible world in which I would not exist. It represents my non-existence, not by including the proposition that I do not exist but simply by omitting me. That I would not exist if all the propositions it includes, and no other actual propositions, were true is not a fact internal to the world that it describes, but an observation that we make from our vantage point in the actual world...

> Let us mark this difference in point of view by saying that the proposition that I never exist... is true *at* many possible worlds, but *in* none (Adams [5], p. 22).

Fine's inner truth or Adams truth-in is the ordinary notion of truth in a world that we see from Plantinga [101]. Let's call this sense of truth "truth inside a world."[3] We can define it as follows.

T_I: A proposition p is **true inside** a world W just if necessarily, if W is actual, p is true.

We aren't, however, given an analysis of Fine's outer truth or Adams' truth-at, which we will call "truth outside a world." (We will return to this lack of analysis momentarily.) Rather, we're given a sort of picture to operate with. We evaluate the truth of a proposition from our perspective in the actual world and ask if it is true, regardless of whether it exists there.

How do proponents of the distinction between truth inside a world and truth outside a world think that the distinction bears on our argument? They maintain that there is an ambiguity in (2). (2) can be read either as:

(2') Necessarily, if it is possible Socrates doesn't exist, then the proposition *Socrates does not exist* **is true inside** some possible world.

(2") Necessarily, if it is possible Socrates doesn't exist, then the proposition *Socrates does not exist* **is true outside** some possible world.

The metaphysician who avails herself of the truth inside/outside distinction may maintain that (2') is false. And, while (2") is true, it conjoined with (1) doesn't validly yield (3); for (3) is a claim about truth inside a world. So, either way the modified Plantingan argument is unsound.

At first, our intuitions may balk at the claim that *Socrates does not exist* is not true *simpliciter* if the world in question W (where Socrates doesn't exist) is actual. But we are meant to see that it's *almost true*, or *sort-of true*; *Socrates does not exist* is true *outside* W. And that is supposed to be enough to satisfy the intuition that it's possible that Socrates not exist.

There have been a number of attempts to say what outside truth is. For instance, we find Robert Stalnaker saying:

> [Outside truth], in the relevant sense, is just entailment: a proposition is true with respect to a given possible state of the world if and only if that proposition is entailed by the maximal proposition that is that possible state of the world (Stalnaker [128], p. 31).

I think we can see that this won't work. Consider a world W where Socrates doesn't exist. Suppose we think of W as a maximal proposition. Suppose also we adopt serious actualism, as we do with (4) in our modified Plantingan argument. Does W entail the proposition *Socrates does not exist*? No, because, it's not the case that necessarily, if W is actual, *Socrates does not exist* is true. If W is actual, *Socrates does not exist* doesn't itself exist. The existentialist may reply: "Yes, it's not true *inside* W. But it is *outside* W." That's fine so far as it goes, but it's not something Stalnaker can say here. He's trying to tell us what outside truth is and can't appeal to it in giving an account of it.

It might be tempting to give an analysis of outside truth in terms of states of affairs that obtain or properties that are exemplified in or "inside" W. The problem with this, of course, is that the motivation the existentialist has for thinking *Socrates does not exist* is not true inside W will apply to any quidditative state of affairs or property. In order to give a proper analysis of a singular proposition's being true outside a world in terms of some other abstract object obtaining inside or being instantiated inside a world; the thing the singular proposition is

92 Haecceity and Existence

about must show up, quidditatively, in the *analysans*. When that happens, the proponent of the inside/outside truth distinction will face questions about the existence of this new abstract object which was to do the grounding for the fact that the singular proposition was true outside the world in question. If it can hold inside W, why doesn't *Socrates does not exist* exist inside W? (This objection will resurface when considering premise (5).)

Jason Turner [134] gives the following conditions for a non-modal proposition *p*'s being true outside a world W. He takes each to give sufficient conditions for *p*'s being true outside W, and the disjunction of the conditions in each of the three to be necessary for p to be true outside W.

(C1) If *p* is true [inside] W, then *p* is true [outside] W.
(C2) If *p*="~E!(*a*)," *w* is W's world description, and *a* is not a constituent of *w*, then *p* is true [outside] W.[4]
(C3) If a proposition *p* follows in a negative free logic from propositions true [outside] W, then *p* is true [outside] W.

(C2) will be the condition we are most concerned with here, for we seek an account of what it is for the proposition *Socrates does not exist* to be true outside a world W. Turner thinks of world descriptions as maximal propositions that describe what happens in a world. In (C2), Turner is availing himself of the notion of *a*'s being a constituent of the world description in question, *w*. Let's suppose that *a* in this case is Socrates. If in the actual world α, Socrates is not a constituent of the world description *w*; then the proposition *Socrates is not a constituent of w* will be true in α. What is the alethic status of this new proposition, *Socrates is not a constituent of w*? First, we can note that it is to be true inside α. Its truth inside α, the actual world, is supposed to allow it to make *Socrates does not exist* true outside W. Second, we can note that it too is true outside W. Like the proposition *Socrates does not exist*, it won't exist if W is actual. But both accurately characterize W, from our perspective in α. What makes it the case that it is true outside W? We don't have an account in (C2), as (C2) is about negative existential propositions. I suspect Turner would say that it is true outside W because it follows from the proposition *Socrates does not exist*, which is true outside W. An initial concern here might be that the order of explanation is supposed to go the other way round; the proposition about constituenthood in a world story is supposed to explain the outside truth of the negative existential. Perhaps though we could appeal to something else true inside α to explain the truth outside of W of the proposition *Socrates is not a constituent of w*: *Socrates is not a constituent of w is not a constituent of w*. This would give us an account of how, from our perspective in α, various things are true of W.

Haecceity and Existence 93

I think we can see that the disjunction of (C1)–(C3) are not necessary for truth outside a world, though. Consider again the case of Sib. We know Sib doesn't exist in α. Suppose Sib also doesn't exist in W. Then the proposition *Sib does not exist* should be true outside W; it accurately characterizes W from our vantage point in α. But the existentialist presumably must say *Sib is not a constituent of w* is not true inside α, for it doesn't exist in α. So, *Sib does not exist* being true outside W is not via (C2). *Sib does not exist* also is not true inside W, as it doesn't exist inside W.[5] Thus, the outside truth of *Sib does not exist* at W is not via (C1). Nor does it follow from a proposition true outside W in a negative free logic; thus, *Sib does not exist* is not true outside W via (C3). Thus, the outside truth of *Sib does not exist* must be explained by some means other than those we find in (C1)–(C3). So, the disjunction of conditions in (C1)–(C3) are not necessary for truth outside a world. Thus, we don't have from Turner an account of truth outside a world.

Jeff Speaks [127] attempts to give an analysis of truth outside a world in terms of worlds, in α, having quidditative truth conditions. He construes these truth conditions as properties. The idea is that W actually has the property *being such that if W is actual Socrates does not exist*. This is supposed to secure that *Socrates does not exist* is true outside W. Why? Because were W actual, Socrates would not exist. I have two concerns about this proposal. First, it too has trouble with the Sib case. *Sib does not exist* should be true outside W. But W doesn't in α have the truth condition *being such that if W is actual, Sib does not exist*. Why? This truth condition is a quidditative property. If it can exist inside W, why can't *Socrates does not exist* exist inside W?

Second, note that Speaks' truth conditions are "object-level" and don't involve propositions. So, he's *not* saying that W has the truth condition *being such that were W actual, the proposition Socrates does not exist would be true*. But he does accept that the condition Socrates does not exist would hold if W were actual. But surely W would record this fact with abstracta of some kind—a proposition, presumably—were W actual. How can the condition in the consequent of the truth condition hold inside the world if the requisite proposition isn't true inside the world? Perhaps the idea is that the condition holds outside the world. But then we're clearly not giving a reductive analysis of outside truth, for we're invoking outside truth in the analysis.

I suspect there is no non-circular reductive account of truth outside a world (see Davidson [39, 43]). The concept may be a perfectly good one, of course. Maybe there just isn't a reductive analysis of it, though we understand it and find it useful to employ. But it would be good to have an analysis of what it is. It is much more complex than other potential primitives for which we may not seek analyses (e.g. modality, truth, existence). Thus,

94 Haecceity and Existence

it seems like the sort of thing that should have an analysis, in the way that truth inside a world has an analysis.

Let us see if there is another way to reject our modified Plantingan argument for unexemplified haecceities, then. We turn to premise (4).

(4) Necessarily, if *Socrates does not exist* is true, *Socrates does not exist* exists.

One reason to think that (4) is true is because of a commitment to serious actualism, the claim that only existing things can exemplify properties or stand in relations. Serious actualism has been defended by a number of people, including Alvin Plantinga [103, 104] and Michael Bergmann [15]. However, even if my rejection of serious actualism in [47] is correct, (4) will look plausible to those who think that something must exist to be true. (As we noted before, we may allow that objects that don't exist may exemplify properties and stand in relations without holding that they may exemplify every property or stand in every relation.[6]) But for those who reject serious actualism and will allow propositions to be true or false at a world though they don't exist at that world, (4) will be rejected.

Premise (5) will have appeal to the serious actualist who thinks that haecceities are constituents of singular propositions. If *being Socrates* is a constituent of *Socrates does not exist*, then *being Socrates* must exist. There are a number of ways by which one may reject (5), however. For instance, one might deny that propositions have constituents. Or, one might think that singular propositions do have constituents, but don't have haecceities as constituents. Or, suppose one thinks that singular propositions have haecceities as constituents, yet may exist even if the haecceity that is a constituent of them doesn't exist. This might be because one thinks that the singular proposition doesn't have its constituents essentially or that it does have its constituents essentially, and a nonexistent haecceity may stand in the requisite propositional formation relations to have a complete proposition. Either of these views will lead to rejection of (5).

Suppose, though, that one is a serious actualist who thinks that haecceities are constituents of singular propositions (e.g. Plantinga himself). Then the modified Plantingan argument looks like a good argument. If we maintain that the truth inside/outside distinction is untenable, we lose the means to reject (2). Serious actualism will get us the truth of (4). If one thinks that haecceities are constituents of singular propositions, then it is very hard to see how the serious actualist rejects (5). Even if the serious actualist doesn't think that haecceities are constituents of propositions (perhaps propositions are primitive entities or sets of worlds), there will be some pressure for the believer in haecceities to accept the existence of quidditative properties like *being Socrates* once she accepts the existence of *Socrates does not exist*. (It may be that the pressure comes directly from accepting

Haecceity and Existence 95

the negative singular proposition, or via the existence of negative quidditative properties like *being distinct from Socrates*, and then from the argument from negative quidditative properties in Section 4.1.2 to the existence of *being Socrates*.) Once we have the first five premises, we validly arrive at (6). This modified Plantingan argument for unexemplified haecceities then will hold appeal to the serious actualist who thinks that haecceities are constituents of singular propositions.

In Section 5.1, we have examined four arguments for the possibility of unexemplified haecceities. Though there is room for rejecting each of them, I find the semantic argument from Section 5.1.3 compelling. Thus, I think there is reason to think that there are unexemplified haecceities. Indeed, we have the same sort of case to think that there are unexemplified haecceities as there is to think that there are haecceities in the first place.

So much then for arguments that there can be unexemplified haecceities. We turn now to arguments *against* the possibility of unexemplified haecceities.

5.2 Arguments that Haecceities Depend for Their Existence on the Objects that Instantiate Them

5.2.1 An Argument from Constituentism

To this point in the chapter, we have not said anything about the nature of haecceities beyond their being properties that are capable of being exemplified. Given the truth of constituentism about haecceities (rather than primitivism), we have a straightforward argument against the possibility of there being unexemplified haecceities. Consider a world W where Socrates doesn't exist. Could Socrates' haecceity, *being Socrates*, exist there? It would seem not, for Socrates does not exist in W to be a constituent of the haecceity *being Socrates*. There is then *prima facie* pressure away from accepting unexemplified haecceities if one is a constituentist.

What should the constituentist say? The first thing she might say is that the objector is right; there are no unexemplified haecceities. This would not be a strange move for the constituentist to make: If haecceities have contingent objects as constituents, then the haecceity exists only if the object does.

Suppose, though, that the constituentist wants to hold onto unexemplified haecceities. There are two things that she might then say. First, she might say that though *being Socrates* has Socrates as a constituent, it doesn't *essentially* have Socrates as a constituent. Thus, *being Socrates* may exist even though it doesn't have Socrates as a constituent. Thus, it can exist in worlds where Socrates doesn't exist. Second, she might adopt independence actualism and say that though *being Socrates* does essentially have Socrates as a constituent, Socrates may stand in the requisite property compositional relations to be a constituent of *being Socrates* even when Socrates doesn't exist. The second solution seems preferable to the first; surely if Socrates is a constituent of *being Socrates*, *being Socrates* has Socrates as a constituent essentially. Thus, if one is going to be a constituentist and is inclined to accept unexemplified haecceities, one will be pushed in the direction of independence actualism. Or, if one is a serious actualist and finds the arguments in Section 5.1 convincing, one is pushed away from constituentism.

5.2.2 Arguments from Robert Adams

Consider the following passage from Robert Adams' "Primitive Thisness and Primitive Identity."

> It is hard to see how an actualist could consistently maintain that there is a thisness of a non-actual individual. For if there were one, it would be the property of being identical with that individual. To be the property of being identical with a particular individual is to stand, primitively, in a unique relation with that individual...[M]y thisness could not exist without being mine...So if there were a thisness of a non-actual individual, it would stand, primitively, in a relation to that individual. But according to actualism non-actual individuals cannot enter primitively into any relation. It seems to follow that according to actualism, there cannot be a thisness of a non-actual individual (Adams [5], p. 11).

There are at least two arguments against unexemplified haecceities here. We see the first when we note his use of "thisness" in place of "haecceity." If one thinks of an haecceity is the property of *being this thing*, how could there be such a property if there isn't the thing in question? How can there be a thisness if there is no this? A thisness is sort of like an haecceity trope in this regard.

There is a second, similar argument we can take from Adams' text. This is that an haecceity essentially stands in a relation to the individual it is about, and serious actualism says that anything that stands in a relation exists. Now, one may argue that this relationship is the this-thisness relationship just discussed. But one might think that it holds even if one isn't thinking of haecceities in terms of thisnesses. An haecceity is a unique sort of property, primitively tied to the individual who exemplifies it. That sort of property might be thought to be dependent on the existence of the individual who exemplifies it.

What should we say about Adams' arguments here? Let's begin with the first argument we take from Adams. Consider the haecceity of the table I'm writing at, *being this table in front of me*. Adams asks, how could this property exist if the table didn't? Well, what precisely is the problem with it existing even though the table doesn't? Maybe I couldn't grasp the haecceity if the table didn't exist. Furthermore, maybe if I could grasp it, I wouldn't denote it with "being this table in front of me." There are, of course, many different gerund phrases with which I can pick out the same haecceity. Perhaps if we are thinking of a thisness as a sort of trope—an instantiated haecceity—then *that* couldn't exist without the table existing. But of course the instantiation of *being this table in front of me* is the table, and its self-dependence doesn't give us any reason to think its haecceity, *qua* property, can't exist without the table. So I don't see that this first argument from Adams gives us any reason to think that haecceities can't exist unexemplified. To be fair to Adams, he's not here giving a rigorous argument for the object-dependence of haecceities. Rather, he is pointing to the relation between haecceity and object and hoping that you will have his intuitions that the haecceity needs the object.

The second argument from Adams is that haecceities are essentially related to the object they are haecceities of. But this is just to assert that haecceities can't exist unexemplified and as such doesn't serve as an independent reason for thinking they can't. As with the argument in Section 5.1, an independence actualist may deny that standing in the sort of primitive relation between a thing and haecceity claimed essential here entails the existence of the relata. So even if one insists that the haecceity needs to stand in relations to the object it is an haecceity of, there is conceptual room to argue that it can do so even if that object doesn't exist.

5.2.3 The Tantamount-to-Possibilism Objection

A fourth argument against the possibility of unexemplified haecceities has the following structure: If one accepts unexemplified haecceities, one is accepting nonexistent objects into her ontology. But actualism is true. Thus, there are no unexemplified haecceities. The criticism is that with a view like Plantinga's [105], unexemplified haecceities play much the same role that nonexistent possible objects do on a Meinongian view. Indeed, in the (Plantinga-endorsed) semantics for the metaphysics from Plantinga [105], Jager [73] uses necessarily existing essences in place of the stock of *possibilia* one gets from variable domain Kripke models. Alan McMichael [92] makes just this criticism of Plantinga:

> This objection to unexemplified Haecceities is no isolated intuition. Once Plantinga's Haecceitism is fully spelled out, we can see that it bears a striking structural resemblance to the possibilist theories we have rejected. In place of every nonactual possible object, there stands an unexemplified Haecceity. Indeed, Plantinga's Haecceitist semantics is isomorphic to the usual

Kripke semantics. The Kripke semantics is, on the face of it, a possibilist semantics, since we can identify within it a set of all possible objects, actual and nonactual.

This isomorphism is one of the signs that Plantinga is having trouble with the actualist program. Another sign is that he has departed from the usual actualist basis. Typically, the actualist reduces worlds to existing individuals, general properties, and general relations. To introduce primitive properties each of which is specific to some nonactual object seems tantamount to acceptance of possibilism. Yet, this is precisely what Plantinga does (McMichael [92], p. 61).[7]

Christopher Menzel makes the same sort of criticism of Plantinga's view:

A traditional platonic understanding of properties - I would argue the dominant one - is that, at the most basic level, properties are what diverse but similar particulars have in common. That properties are, in the first instance, general, they are universals. But on this understanding there seems no justification for purely nonqualitative essences at all, since they are neither general themselves, nor logic compounds of general properties and relations. There is little enough to distinguish purely nonqualitative essences from concrete possibilia save a thin actualist veneer. In light of this understanding of properties that too is stripped away, and haecceitism of this variety collapses into possibilism (Menzel [93], p. 366).

What about this fourth argument against unexemplified haecceities—that this view collapses into possibilism? Let us grant the assumption that we ought to hold onto actualism. It is true that in the formal semantics for Plantinga's view in Jager [73], there is an isomorphism between possible objects and individual essences. But this fact doesn't make Plantinga's own metaphysics in places like Plantinga [101] and Plantinga [105] possibilistic. There are no nonexistent objects on Plantinga's view. That is, in the scope of Plantinga's widest quantifiers, there are only things that exist. Furthermore, names like "Vulcan" and "Sib" are empty on Plantinga's account. (They have as semantic contents an essence, but don't refer to one.) On a possibilist account, these names *would* refer, and that reference would be to nonexistent objects. So, it's quite clear that a view like Plantinga's on which there are unexemplified haecceities that go proxy in some ways for nonexistent objects doesn't need to be Meinongian, *pace* McMichael and Menzel.

5.2.4 Conclusion

I don't think that any of the four arguments we've considered in this section give us reason to think that there can't be unexemplified haecceities. Furthermore, we have some promising arguments for the existence of unexemplified haecceities that we saw in the first part of the chapter. If we are independence actualists, the semantic argument from Section 5.1.3 gives us reason to think that there can be unexemplified haecceities. If we are serious actualists, there are at least two other arguments that give us reason to think that there can be unexemplified haecceities. Thus, I conclude that there is reason for believing in the possibility of unexemplified haecceities.[8]

In the next chapter, we turn to the epistemology of haecceity. Are there good reasons to think that we aren't able to grasp haecceities of ordinary objects around us? We will consider arguments for and against our ability to grasp these haecceities.

Notes

1. Some of the content in this chapter overlaps ch. 6 of my [47].
2. I discuss the case of Sib in my [47]; it is a variation on Nathan Salmon's Noman case [121].
3. I want to use something closer to Fine's language to mark this concept because in ordinary possible worlds discourse "in" and "at" are often used interchangeably.
4. He defines "E! " as follows: E!(a) is true if $\exists x(x=a)$.
5. We continue to assume the truth of serious actualism at this point in the argument. The inside/outside truth distinction is not supposed to rest on the denial of serious actualism.
6. For one, they won't exemplify *existence*.
7. Note that "Haecceitism," as McMichael uses it, is Plantinga's view that there are necessarily existing haecceities. It is not the supervenience claim, "haecceitism" (see the Introduction for a definition).
8. The issue of the contingent existence of haecceities is part of a larger issue around the contingent existence of abstracta. On this larger issue; in addition to work cited in this chapter (particularly Plantinga [101, 108] and Stalnaker [129]), I refer the reader to Williamson [141], Fritz and Goodman [56], Fritz [55], and Fine's postscript in [114].

6 Haecceity and Acquaintance

Over the past 50 years, there has been a robust discussion concerning our acquaintance with haecceities. A number of philosophers have argued that the class of haecceities with which we are acquainted is not a broad one. In particular, they argue that we are not able to grasp the haecceities of ordinary material objects in our environment. Our inability to grasp haecceities may have theoretical virtues. In particular, suppose we think of haecceities as constituents of propositions. Then, that there are ungraspable haecceities may help to explain how my *de se* beliefs differ from yours (Chisholm [25]) or a manner by which God's knowledge differs from ours (Wierenga [140]).

In this chapter, I want to examine the issue of our acquaintance with haecceities. In the first part of the chapter, I will consider in greater depth what it is to be acquainted with haecceities. In the second part of the chapter, I will consider an argument from Jonathan Kvanvig that our powers of acquaintance with haecceities are significant. I will argue that though the target of Kvanvig's argument—Roderick Chisholm—has a reply to his argument, the constituentist does not. In the last part of the chapter, I will consider an argument from Gary Rosenkrantz that our powers of acquaintance with haecceities are limited. I will argue, *pace* Rosenkrantz, that we are able to grasp the haecceities of ordinary material objects. In addition, I will argue we are able to grasp haecceities of abstract objects that we can think about.

6.1 Concerning Acquaintance with Haecceities

Before we ask whether we are acquainted with haecceities, it is important to ask what sorts of things haecceities are. For instance, if hylomorphic partism about haecceities is correct, the mechanism of our acquaintance with haecceities may well involve Aristotelian abstraction of forms in sense perception. If haecceities are properties in the way the primitivist or constituentist claims, acquaintance with haecceities will involve the grasping of properties. In this book, I am defending *sui generis* constituentism, so we will consider principally the question of our acquaintance with haecceities given that they are properties with individuals as constituents.

We will seek, then, to ask whether we can grasp haecceities that are properties with individuals as constituents. This leads to a more general question: What is it to grasp a property? Sometimes talk of grasping properties suggests quasi-Gödellian occult mental faculties that involve perception of abstracta.[1] But I don't think we need to think of the grasping of properties in this way. To grasp a property is just to think about it and in doing so to form (true) beliefs about what would have to be the case were it exemplified. Even noting this, there remains the question of how I can think about an abstract object. But there also remains the question of how *any* sort of mental intentionality works. I am inclined to think that there is no reductive analysis of mental intentionality; thus, the difficulty we have in accounting for our ability to think about abstracta is part of a larger difficulty accounting for our ability to think about things in general. Somehow causal relations have something to do with my ability to think of ordinary material objects. Yet, even for concrete objects, mental intentionality doesn't reduce to causal relations, as causal relations are not fine-grained enough to capture what we think about in the material world. A book on haecceity is not the place to assess theories of intentionality, however. It suffices for our purposes here to note that we do grasp properties and that our doing so involves thinking of them and forming beliefs about their instantiation conditions.

Suppose, then, that haecceities have objects that exemplify them as constituents. Thus, an haecceity like *being this desk* has my desk as a constituent. On this picture of haecceities, can we see a way by which we may grasp them? I think we can. Consider the case of *being this desk*. Right now, I am thinking about my desk. Indeed, I am perceptually acquainted with my desk. It is brown and grainy and cool to the touch. But then, surely I can grasp the property *being this desk*. At the present moment, I am thinking about the property *being this desk*; I am able to sensorily perceive and think about the desk, the same desk which is a constituent of *being this desk*. Furthermore, I know what would be the case were *being this desk* instantiated; this desk (pointing at the desk) that I'm looking at would exist. As a result, I can grasp the desk's haecceity, *being this desk*.[2] Thus, we have a model for the grasping of the haecceities of material objects in my environment.

What about other sorts of haecceities? Consider the case of Socrates. The haecceity *being Socrates* has a constituent that I'm not perceptually acquainted with. Am I able to grasp *being Socrates*? It seems that I can. I am able to think about Socrates; I am doing so right now. I know what would be the case if the property *being Socrates* were instantiated: Socrates—that entity I'm thinking about right now—would exist. Thus, I don't see a reason

102   Haecceity and Acquaintance

to deny that I can grasp haecceities of material objects with which I am not perceptually acquainted.

The same sort of reasoning will apply to my grasping of haecceities of abstract objects. *Being the number three* has as a constituent the number three. I am able to think about the number three; I'm doing so right now. Furthermore, I know what would be the case were *being the number three* to be instantiated: The number three would exist. Thus, it seems that I can grasp haecceities of some abstract objects, as well.

I conclude that the constituentist has available to her the outlines of an epistemology for the grasping of haecceities. It is parasitic on our ability to think about things that are the constituents of the haecceities in question. Once we have the object in mind, we can deduce instantiation conditions for the haecceity in question: that the object in mind would exist. In the absence of serious arguments against the possibility of grasping the haecceities of ordinary material objects and some abstracta, the constituentist is *prima facie* justified in thinking that we can grasp the haecceities of these objects.

We turn to two extant arguments concerning our ability to grasp haecceities. The first from Jonathan Kvanvig purports to show that we can grasp many, if not all, haecceities. The second from Gary Rosenkrantz purports to show that we cannot grasp the haecceities of the objects around us.

6.2   A Kvanvigian Argument against "The Haecceity Theory"

Jonathan Kvanvig gives an argument against what he calls "The Haecceity Theory."[3] The Haecceity Theory is a theory about the metaphysics of propositions and our ability to grasp them. There are two key elements to The Haecceity Theory, which is most thoroughly explicated and defended by Roderick Chisholm in *Person and Object* [25]. The first element is that haecceities are constituents of propositions. The second is that we are unable to grasp haecceities of most objects that we might refer to. The conjunction of these two elements yields the existence of propositions that are ungraspable by most people. Consider the following sentence,

(S1)   I am cold.

If I utter (use) (S1), it expresses a proposition with my haecceity in it, which we may represent with (P1).

(P1)   <my haecceity, *being cold*>.

If you utter (S1), however, (S1) expresses a proposition with your haecceity in it.

(P2)   <your haecceity, *being cold*>.

Haecceity and Acquaintance 103

I am able to grasp my own haecceity; as a result, I can grasp (P1). I am unable to grasp your haecceity, however. As a result, I am not able to grasp (P2). The existence of these perspectivally-limited propositions is used by defenders of The Haecceity Theory explain how my *de se* beliefs differ from your *de se* beliefs.

Kvanvig gives an argument against The Haecceity Theory. It proceeds as follows. Call the haecceity of Ronald Reagan R. According to The Haecceity Theory, only Reagan can grasp R. As a result, only Reagan can grasp propositions which have R as a constituent. Then, the proponent of The Haecceity Theory claims that:

(K) R is such that only Reagan can grasp propositions which have R as a constituent

is true.

We are able to grasp the proposition expressed by (K), however. So either (i) we must be able to grasp R, or (ii) R isn't, after all, a constituent of the proposition expressed by (K). The Haecceity Theorist denies both of these claims. Thus, either (i) or (ii) is a problem for the Haecceity Theorist.

How should someone like Chisholm who defends The Haecceity Theory respond to Kvanvig's argument? I think that Chisholm should deny that R is a part of the proposition expressed by (K). To see how this sort of reply might work, consider my utterance of (S1) above. The Haecceity Theorist thinks that the proposition that it expresses contains my haecceity as a constituent. We have a term in the sentence (S1), "I", whose referent is me and whose semantic content is my haecceity.

Now consider (K). It contains a term, "R", whose referent is an haecceity. It is easy here to confuse levels of sense and reference, so let's refer to Reagan's haecceity as *being Reagan*. We then may rewrite (K) for sake of clarity.

(K') *Being Reagan* is such that only Reagan can grasp propositions which have *being Reagan* as a constituent.

Then Kvanvig claims: Either *being Reagan* is part of the proposition expressed by (K'), and we can grasp *being Reagan* (for we can grasp (K')); or *being Reagan* isn't part of the proposition expressed by (K'). Either is a problem for The Haecceity Theorist.

It now seems clear what The Haecceity Theorist should say about Kvanvig's argument. In (S1), "I" has as its referent me and its semantic content my haecceity. Then in (K'), "*being Reagan*" has as its referent an haecceity and its semantic content an haecceity of an haecceity, *being being Reagan*. While it is part of The Haecceity Theorist's view that I cannot grasp *being Reagan*, it is *not* part of The Haecceity Theorist's view that we can't grasp haecceities of abstracta like the haecceity of Reagan's haecceity. We don't need to be able to grasp Reagan's haecceity in order to grasp the propositions expressed by (K) or (K'); we need only to be able to grasp Reagan's haecceity's haecceity. Thus, someone like Chisholm has a reply to Kvanvig's argument. Chisholm may hold onto perspectivally-limited propositions and The Haecceity Theory, at least in the face of this particular attack.

There is a reply that Kvanvig might make to this reply to his argument. As we saw in Chapter 1; when he believes in haecceities, Roderick Chisholm is a primitivist about haecceities. Suppose one were a constituentist, however. Then, the haecceity of Reagan's haecceity has Reagan's haecceity as a constituent. Then, it seems that in order to grasp the haecceity of Reagan's haecceity, I need to be able to grasp Reagan's haecceity. Thus, our reply to Kvanvig on behalf of The Haecceity Theorist won't ultimately work if constituentism is true. In order to grasp the proposition expressed by (K'), I *do* need to be able to grasp Reagan's haecceity.

I think this last bit of reasoning is sound, so I'm inclined to think that Kvanvig's argument is a good argument provided that one, unlike Chisholm, is a constituentist. If we consider the simpler sentence:

(L) *Being Reagan* is an haecceity

we can see why this would be. The primitivist can say that the proposition expressed by (L) doesn't have *being Reagan* as a constituent. (It has, rather, *being being Reagan*.) However, for the constituentist, the proposition expressed by (L) *does* have *being Reagan* as a constituent. If we grant the plausible assumption that to grasp a proposition is to grasp its constituents, Kvanvig's argument has bite against The Haecceity Theorist who is a constituentist.

Thus, the philosopher who is the person that Kvanvig has in mind when he speaks of the defender of The Haecceity Theory—Roderick Chisholm—has a reply to Kvanvig's argument. But a constituentist doesn't have a reply; for the constituentist, it seems that we have the ability to grasp all sorts of haecceities. I like this result; as I argued in Section 6.1, I think that the constituentist has a model on which we are able to grasp many haecceities. Indeed, Kvanvig's reasoning may be seen as a strength of constituentism; if constituentism is true, we have clever argument that yields the conclusion that we can grasp many haecceities.

There is an important argument that we *cannot* grasp the haecceities of ordinary objects in our environment (like Reagan), though. We turn to it now.

6.3 The Argument from Reidentification

The principal argument against our grasping haecceities of ordinary material objects is what I will call *the argument from reidentification*. The basic thrust of the argument is this: If we can grasp haecceities of ordinary material objects, we can reidentify the objects across time merely by grasping their haecceities and comparing them. We cannot reidentify objects in this way; therefore, we cannot grasp the haecceities of ordinary material objects. The most thorough statement of this sort of argument is from Gary Rosenkrantz in chapter 5 of his book *Haecceity: An Ontological Essay*. There are echoes of it elsewhere, however. In *Person and Object*, Chisholm takes up the question of whether the way we pick out other individuals is different from the way we pick out ourselves (Chisholm [25], pp. 34–36). As part of this argument he considers the fact that thought we may be wrong in reidentifying other objects, we cannot be wrong in reidentifying ourselves. He credits Rosenkrantz with this observation (Chisholm [25], p. 200, n. 24). Rosenkrantz himself finds hints of the argument from reidentification in a 1951 book by Peter C. Vier, *Evidence and Its Function According to Scotus*:

> "Sincere truth," [Scotus] writes, "is not grasped by the senses in such wise as to enable them to perceive the immutability of the truth they apprehend, or for this matter, the immutability itself of the object. For the senses perceive present objects only as long as these are present..." Even supposing that I should have the object A uninterruptedly in my presence, and that I should gaze upon it without intermission, so that my vision would retain the same grade of sharpness throughout the whole process, I would still be unable to perceive the immutability of A, for at each moment of my vision I would perceive the object precisely as it is constituted at that same moment (Vier [139], p. 154).[4]

Vier seems to be saying that it is consistent with my sensory experience that objects I perceive not persist through time. That seems right. That we can be wrong in our beliefs about the persistence of objects distinct from us is at the core of Rosenkrantz's argument from reidentification.

To see how Rosenkrantz develops the argument, let us begin with Rosenkrantz's definition of acquaintance.

> (D3) S is acquainted with x =df (i) x exemplifies the haecceity, being identical with N, and (ii) S knows that there is something that is N, and in knowing this grasps x's haecceity (Rosenkrantz [117], p. 187).

Acquaintance, then, involves the grasping of haecceities. We then can state Rosenkrantz's rendering of the argument from reidentification.

> (1) If perceiving a physical object or person enables any one of us to be acquainted with it, then he has the ability to identify

an object x he presently perceives with an object y he perceived earlier, by grasping the haecceities of x and y, comparing them, and seeing they are the same.

(2) None of us has such an ability.

Therefore,

(3) Perceiving a physical object or person does not enable any of us to be acquainted with it (Rosenkrantz [117], pp. 192–193).[5]

To get from our not being acquainted with physical objects (which is what (3) gets us) to our not grasping haecceities requires negating (ii) of (D3). (Rosenkrantz has already argued that (i) is true of material objects and people.) If (ii) of (D3) is false, then it surely must be that S doesn't grasp x's haecceity.

When evaluating the main argument from Rosenkrantz, the first thing one wants to know is why (2) is true; why don't we have the ability to compare haecceities across time? To motivate (2), Rosenkrantz gives a thought experiment (Rosenkrantz [117], pp. 200–201). We are to imagine a friend, Mo, who displays two qualitatively identical similar objects. (We can suppose they are red rubber balls.) Mo puts the rubber balls behind his back where we can't see them. Then Mo displays one of the two balls. Call this ball o1. Mo puts o1 behind his back and a minute later displays one of the two balls from behind his back. Call this second ball o2. Suppose that o1=o2. Rosenkrantz claims that we are unable to know this. Why is this? Rosenkrantz claims that if we are able to reidentify objects via haecceity; then if o1=o2, we know that o1=o2. However, we don't know o1=o2 because the justification we have for believing it is undercut by the sufficiently high likelihood that o1≠o2.

In the rubber ball scenario, it is clear we are doing little more than guessing as to whether o1 is o2. That we would be guessing is an empirical fact; even the defender of our ability to grasp the haecceities of ordinary material objects would have to grant that a counterfactual scenario in which someone showed us a series of two qualitatively exactly similar objects and asked us to judge identity or distinctness of the objects would involve our being wrong roughly half the time. But what we don't get from Rosenkrantz is an argument why our grasping the haecceities of o1 and o2 is inconsistent with our being wrong in our beliefs about the identity or distinctness of o1 and o2. Why should we expect our ability to discern identity or distinctness of haecceities to be any better than our ability to discern identity or distinctness of objects? This is a key premise in Rosenkrantz's argument, and we find no support for it from Rosenkrantz.[6]

I think that any sort of haecceity theorist has this sort of retort to Rosenkrantz available to her. But I think that the constituentist has a particularly strong reply to Rosenkrantz's argument. For any haecceity theorist who thinks haecceities are properties, to grasp an haecceity is just to think about it, and in doing so to form true beliefs about what would be the case were it instantiated. The constituentist holds that what would be the case were the haecceity instantiated is that the object which is a constituent of the haecceity would exist. Forming beliefs about this, however, has no implication for our ability to distinguish haecceities at different times. Indeed, the constituentist should expect it to be just as difficult to diachronically tell haecceities of qualitative exactly similar objects apart as it is to tell the objects apart themselves. Grasping the haecceities won't give us any special powers of discernment of identity or non-identity.

Could Rosenkrantz defend the claim that we have better access to facts about identity or distinctness of haecceities than we do facts about identity or distinctness of material objects? I don't see how such an argument would go, even for a primitivist about haecceity. Furthermore, we have just seen that this claim looks to be false for a constituentist about haecceity. Thus, I conclude that Rosenkrantz's argument from reidentification does not succeed. The argument rests on the unsupported claim about the epistemology of haecceity that acquaintance with an haecceity is tied to our ability to reidentify it. The argument then doesn't give us reason to think that we don't grasp the haecceities of ordinary material objects.

Furthermore, we noted in the first part of the chapter that there is reason to think that we do grasp the haecceities of material objects and abstracta. Moreover, if we are constituentists, Kvanvig's argument also gives us reason to think that we grasp the haecceities of ordinary material objects and abstracta. I conclude, then, that we are justified in thinking that the class of haecceities that we grasp is very broad.

Notes

1 It's not at all clear that Gödel himself embraces occult faculties; see Parsons [99] for discussion. Gödel does however liken mathematical intuition to "a kind of perception" (Parsons [99], p. 65).
2 A reviewer raises a question about this: how am I able to grasp the haecceity of the desk rather than something like the aggregate of wood molecules in the same region of space? Let's grant that there are multiple objects in the desk-shaped region of space. (I'm inclined to think that this is the case, though it is a desk temporal part and a desk, rather than a desk and an aggregate.) Then we have a version of the "*qua* problem." I'm assuming that we have some sort of answer to this problem; any (reductive) theory of reference that is so coarse-grained that we can't refer to the desk rather than (say) an aggregate has to be wrong. I tend to think that there is no reductive account of reference, though

we do refer to things in a fine-grained way (so we are able to refer to the desk rather than the aggregate of wood molecules). When I grasp the haecceity of the desk, rather than the aggregate, I form true beliefs about what would have to be the case if it were instantiated: *that* (ostending the desk) would exist.

3 I'm capitalizing the name of the theory to avoid confusion with other theories about haecceity.

4 Vier does not say where in Scotus the quote comes from. Rosenkrantz attributes the entire quotation and argument above to Scotus; though Scotus' own words stop after "these are present" in the quotation. The parts of the quote most relevant to the argument from reidentification are from Vier rather than Scotus.

5 This is not the final form of his rendering of the argument from reidentification. That argument, which occurs on pp. 194–195, is stated with more technical language. The conceptual machinery of the two arguments are importantly similar, however. As a result, criticisms we make of the above-stated argument will apply to the later, more-technical argument *mutatis mutandis*. For clarity and ease of exposition we will engage with the former, less-technical argument.

6 It is true that in grasping the haecceity of an object, we form true beliefs about what would be the case were the haecceity instantiated: that object would exist. But this says nothing about our ability to reidentify objects over time.

7 Haecceity Applied
Thisness Presentism

In a series of recent works (Ingram [69, 70, 71]), David Ingram defends a view he calls "Thisness Presentism." Thisness Presentism is the conjunction of presentism with Ingram's particular account of haecceity. We saw in Section 2.1.2 that Ingram is a primitivist about haecceity. We also saw in Section 4.4 that Ingram thinks that haecceities and other quidditative properties depend for their existence on the entities that instantiate them, though they may continue to exist after those entities cease to exist.[1] Thus, for Ingram, there are no haecceities of nonactual individuals, nor are there haecceities of future individuals. There are only haecceities of past and present individuals.

In this chapter, I want to examine Ingram's Thisness Presentism and uses to which he puts it to address problems for presentism. Doing so will highlight a number of different ways in which haecceities may be utilized in shoring up and supporting a metaphysical project. We will consider Ingram's application of his metaphysics of haecceities to three problems that arise for the presentist: Having complete singular propositions, grounding cross-time relations, and accounting for temporal passage.

7.1 Application 1: Complete Singular Propositions

The presentist thinks that there are no wholly past or future entities. There seem to be true singular propositions about non-present individuals, however. For instance, it seems that the proposition

(P1) <Socrates was a philosopher>

is a singular proposition that is true now. Socrates (we may so stipulate) is a wholly past entity, however. Thus for the presentist, Socrates isn't now in the scope of our widest quantifiers. This generates what Ingram calls "the constituent problem."

DOI: 10.4324/9781003439738-8

> Presentists face a problem concerning the existence of structured singular propositions about the past. Structured propositions are partly constituted by other entities and depend for their existence upon the existence of such constituents. But, if wholly past entities do not exist, as presentists maintain, what constitutes structured propositions about such past entities? For instance, what constituent can be provided for <Boudica was fierce>? The obvious constituent is Boudica herself. But Boudica does not exist at all, given presentism. And, importantly, this issue generalises for all singular propositions about wholly past entities...Call this the "constituent problem" for presentism (Ingram [71], pp. 87–88).

The constituent problem for presentism, then, is that there are (presently) true singular propositions about wholly past individuals. However, these wholly past individuals—by the presentist's own lights—don't exist.

Ingram himself turns to Thisness Presentism as a solution to the constituent problem. In particular, to solve the constituent problem, Ingram construes haecceities as constituents of singular propositions.[2] Thus, (P1) has as a constituent Socrates' haecceity, *being Socrates*. Though Socrates doesn't exist, his haecceity does. Thus, (P1) isn't lacking any of its constituents now. The presentist then has an account of how a singular proposition about a wholly past individual can exist now and is available to be true or false.

As we consider Ingram's own solution to the constituent problem for presentism, I think that it will be useful to us to have before us a complete (or at least thorough) list of various solutions that a presentist might adopt to the constituent problem. There are at least seven such solutions.

1. **Adopt independence actualism**: The independence actualist will claim that objects that don't exist may nevertheless exemplify properties and stand in relations. The independence actualist could say that (P1) has Socrates as a constituent though Socrates doesn't exist. Socrates, though he doesn't exist, may stand in the requisite propositional compositional relations so that (P1) is a complete proposition. Or, the independence actualist could say that (P1) is true now, though it doesn't exist now.[3]

2. **Deny that propositions have their constituents essentially**: One could say that (P1) only contingently has Socrates as a constituent. Thus, (P1) may exist now, even though it doesn't have Socrates as a constituent. Alongside (2), one presumably also would have to adopt that "gappy" singular propositions are capable of being true (e.g. Braun [21], see Davidson ([47], ch. 3) for discussion.)

3 **Allow singular sentences to change semantic contents and express gappy propositions**: This third strategy is of a similar flavor to the second. On the second strategy, however, the singular proposition expressed by a singular sentence doesn't change when the individual it is about ceases to exist; the same proposition becomes gappy. On this third strategy, the singular sentence comes to express a distinct (though overlapping) gappy proposition.
4 **Reject structured propositions that are built up out of the meanings of the linguistic items that express them**: There are at least three ways one could do this. First, one could reject that there are propositions altogether. Second, one could take propositions to be sets of worlds or functions from worlds to truth values. Third, one could take propositions to be primitive, *sui generis* entities (e.g. Merricks [96]).
5 **Adopt Meinongianism and allow nonexistent entities to be constituents of propositions**: On this strategy, (P1) has Socrates as a constituent. When Socrates exists, Socrates may be a constituent of a singular proposition. Once Socrates ceases to exist, Socrates—now a nonexistent object—may still be a constituent of singular propositions about Socrates.
6 **Allow rigid terms to change semantic contents to haecceities once their referents cease to exist**: On this strategy, so long as Socrates exists, singular sentences with "Socrates" in them express singular propositions with Socrates in them. But once Socrates ceases to exist, the content of "Socrates" becomes Socrates' haecceity, *being Socrates*.
7 **Take all singular propositions to have haecceities (rather than concrete objects) as constituents.**

(7) is Ingram's solution to the constituent problem. Ingram explicitly rejects (4) as a solution to the constituent problem (Ingram [71], p. 88). For Ingram, propositions are structured entities that depend on their components for their existence. Ingram also explicitly rejects (1) as a solution; he is a serious presentist, and if Socrates no longer exists, Socrates cannot be a constituent of a presently existing proposition. Nor can (P1) be true now if it no longer exists.[4] Ingram is an actualist (see endnote 4) and as such will reject solution (5). Ingram finds it implausible that names change their semantic contents when their referent ceases to exist; thus, he explicitly rejects (6) and presumably would reject (3) for the same reason. Ingram thinks that we should accept structured propositions because they are finer-grained than standard set-theoretic conceptions of propositions and also because we may account for structured propositions' representational capacity in a straightforward way. Thus, Ingram will reject (4).[5]

112 Haecceity Applied

Ingram also rejects a view on which a proposition may exist even if its constituents don't; thus, he rejects (2).

I obviously do not have the space to consider here fully the merits of the various replies to the constituent problem.[6] It is worth noting, however, that there is a tension in Ingram's denial of the possibility of unexemplified haecceities and his solution to the constituent problem. To see this, consider again our modified Plantingan argument for unexemplified haecceities from Section 5.1.4.

7.1.1 A Modified Plantingan Argument for the Possibility of Unexemplified Haecceities

1. It is possible Socrates doesn't exist.
2. Necessarily, if it is possible Socrates doesn't exist, then the proposition *Socrates does not exist* is possibly true.
3. Therefore, *Socrates does not exist* is possibly true.
4. Necessarily, if *Socrates does not exist* is true, *Socrates does not exist* exists.
5. Necessarily, if *Socrates does not exist* exists, *being Socrates* exists.
6. Therefore, it is possible that Socrates not exist and *being Socrates* exists.

We saw that the argument has particular bite against the philosopher who thinks that haecceities are constituents of singular propositions. Once one admits the possible truth of *Socrates does not exist*, and one wants to say that it has *being Socrates* as an haecceity; there is pressure to admit the possibility of unexemplified haecceities. Ingram might retreat to a distinction between a proposition's being true inside or outside a world as a reply to this argument. However, as we saw, we have no analysis of the distinction. That there is no analysis of such a conceptually non-basic distinction suggests there is something wrong with it.

There are other ways to reply to the modified Plantingan argument to avoid premise (5), though none of them are available to Ingram. One might say that *Socrates does not exist* does not have constituents or doesn't have its constituents essentially. As we noted, Ingram has rejected both of these as possible replies to the constituent problem; presumably then, he couldn't appeal to them here. Or, one might say *Socrates does not exist* does have its constituents essentially, though it may still exist in worlds where *being Socrates* doesn't exist. This could occur if independence actualism were true and *being Socrates* could stand in the requisite propositional composition relations to *Socrates does not exist* whether or not *being Socrates exists*. As before, Ingram has rejected giving up serious actualism as a response to the constituent problem. If one were to adopt independence actualism in reply to the modified Plantingan argument, one already has a ready reply to the

Haecceity Applied   113

constituent problem: Allow Socrates to be a constituent of (P1) whether or not Socrates exists. Or Ingram could adopt necessitism (Williamson [141]) and say that Socrates, like everything else, is a necessary being. But, there is no constituent problem (or presentism, for that matter) if one is a necessitarian; necessitism is not a view Ingram could accept.

Thus, we can see that Ingram may maintain his solution to the constituent problem and his claim that there can't be unexemplified haecceities only by embracing the truth inside/outside distinction. That this would be the case is perhaps not surprising. Ingram is explicitly drawing from the metaphysics of Robert Adams, and Adams himself employs the distinction.

There are two concerns one might have with Ingram's metaphysics of propositions. The first is that his "singular propositions" are not truly singular propositions. Russellian singular propositions of the sort advocated by people like David Kaplan and Nathan Salmon have concrete individuals as constituents. So (P1) has Socrates himself as a constituent. This yields that the singular proposition is truly "directly about" an individual. A proposition with an haecceity like *being Socrates* may avoid being qualitative in the way a proposition like

(P2) <The ancient snubnosed gadfly was a philosopher>

is. But is (P1) truly a *singular* proposition for Ingram? Defenders of singular propositions may think that it is important for a concrete object to be able to be a constituent of a proposition in order for the proposition to truly be *about* that object. It may be objected that though substituting a non-qualitative haecceity for qualitative properties (as one has in (P2)) is enough to yield a non-qualitative proposition; it isn't enough to result in a true, singular proposition.

A second concern for Ingram's metaphysics of propositions arises when we consider more carefully how he uses it to address the constituent problem. With his view of propositions as structured entities, he is in effect claiming that the semantic contents of rigid terms like "Socrates" are haecceities. Suppose we were to grant that this is the case. Then, a proposition like (P1) would have *being Socrates* as a constituent, rather than Socrates himself.[7] It is surely a contingent fact that the semantic contents of our rigid terms like "Socrates" are haecceities. We could have spoken in a directly referential manner on which the semantic content of "Socrates" would have been the man Socrates himself. Consider a world W where we spoke in a directly referential manner. In W, the proposition (P1) would have Socrates as a constituent. Ingram takes presentism to be a necessary truth (Ingram [71], p. 23). Thus, presentism is true in W. But, then we see that we haven't solved the presentist's problem of singular propositions about past individuals. If we consider times in W after

114 *Haecceity Applied*

which Socrates ceases to exist, we should want to say that (P1) is true. But in W, (P1) at these later times lacks a constituent. How then can it be true?

This sort of problem for Ingram's solution to the constituent problem recurs with Fregean sorts of attempts to solve problems of empty rigid terms. This occurs most illustratively with true negative existential sentences. Consider the sentence

(S1) Vulcan does not exist.

The direct reference theorist is thought to have a problem with (S1) because "Vulcan" is directly referential and thus has Vulcan (if anything) as its semantic content. But, (S1) is true, and thus, "Vulcan" has no semantic content. Thus, (S1) doesn't express a complete proposition. How then can the proposition that (S1) expresses be true? The Fregean will render the semantic content of "Vulcan" as a property/properties that exists whether or not "Vulcan" successfully refers. Thus, the Fregean, it is thought, is in a better position than the direct reference theorist in giving a semantics for a sentence like (S1). The Fregean may appeal to necessarily existing properties to serve as contents for rigid terms.

However, the Fregean in this case will encounter the same sort of problem that Ingram did in his solution to the constituent problem. If our semantics for rigid terms is Fregean, that it is Fregean is a contingent fact. How do we determine whether we speak in a Fregean manner? We consider contingent psychological and linguistic data that points in the direction of belief semantic contents being more fine-grained than referential contents. Perhaps then the Fregean is right about the way we speak, perhaps the contingent psychological and linguistic data point in a Fregean direction. We could have, however, spoken in a directly referential manner. If we had, the propositions expressed by ordinary singular sentences with rigid terms would have been Russellian singular propositions. In the world where we spoke in a directly referential manner, we would again confront the problem of giving truth conditions for a sentence like (S1). This is the case even if we don't have such a problem in the actual world.[8]

Thus, Ingram hasn't solved the constituent problem; at most, he has addressed it in the actual world. To solve the constituent problem, he'd have to argue one of two things: (a) it is a necessary truth that rigid terms express haecceities; or (b) presentism is a contingent truth, and in every world where presentism is true, rigid terms express haecceities. The prospects for either (a) or (b) are dubious. Thus, to truly solve the constituent problem, one will have to adopt one of the other six responses that we considered above.

7.2 Application 2: Presentism and Grounding Past Truths

The presentist thinks that there are no past objects. Yet, there are, presently, truths about the past. That propositions about the past are truths about the past seems to require that there are past objects. Thus, we encounter a *prima facie* problem for the presentist.

There are a wide variety of presentist replies to this problem.[9] Some presentists have responded to this concern by denying that truths about the past need anything to make them true (Merricks [95]). Others have pointed to things that exist presently that can make propositions about the past true. For instance, Thomas Crisp ([35]) and I (Davidson [41], [44]) have suggested that the presentist appeal to abstract times. Abstract times are temporal analogs of the abstract possible worlds of philosophers like Alvin Plantinga ([101, 108]) and Robert Adams ([3]). Consider a proposition like

(P3) <World War II occurred after World War I.>

The defender of the abstract times solution would say that a proposition like (P3) is true because the always existing abstract times represent World War II as occurring after World War I. The details of how exactly this representation works differ from theory to theory. But for the abstract times theorist, there will be at least one primitive tense metric that holds between the times that orders each of them relative to all the other times.

There are other suggestions about to which currently existing entities may allow propositions about the past to be true. For instance, Alan Rhoda grounds truths about the past in divine mental states ([115]). An important suggestion in the context of considering Ingram's own solution to presentist grounding problems is *Lucretianism* (the term is from Bigelow [17]). The standard Lucretian thinks that (P1) is made true by the world's having the property *being such that World War II occurred after World War I*. It's not crucial that the *world* bear this property, however; anything that always exists would do the trick. For instance, Roderick Chisholm [30] has abstract objects bear these sorts of properties. The Lucretian will point to the fact that the instantiation of the property *being such that World War II occurred after World War I* by something (e.g. the world or the number three) will entail the truth of the past proposition (P3).

We may regard Ingram's own Thisness Presentistic solution to grounding past truths as a variety of Lucretianism. He states his solution as follows:

> [F]or any given (true) proposition *p*, about a past entity x, the truth-maker for *p* is a fact that is constituted by X's thisness now instantiating some higher-level past-tensed property that indirectly characterizes x. So, e.g., the truth-maker for [the proposition] <Boudica was fierce> is the fact that Boudica's thisness

116 Haecceity Applied

now instantiates the second-level past-tensed property *having been the thisness of a fierce woman* (Ingram [71], p. 122).

Thus, like Chisholm, Ingram has an abstract object bear the past-directed property. But for Ingram, the bearer of the past-directed property is the haecceity of Boudica. Many Lucretian proposals for grounding past truths are put in terms of a single entity bearing all the past-directed properties (e.g. the world or the number three). Ingram's account has many different bearers of the past-directed properties. Furthermore, the bearer of the past-directed property is the haecceity of Boudica; thus, the property bearer has something to do with the past object that the proposition is about. Sometimes it is claimed that the typical sort of ground that a Lucretian gives for the truth of a proposition like (P1) isn't the right sort of animal to be a ground for (P1). Suppose we take the standard Lucretian tack and say that in grounding (P1) it is the world that bears the property *being such that Socrates was a philosopher*. It is true that if the world instantiates this property (P1) is thereby true. However, one might contend the ground for (P1) should have something to do with Socrates, rather than something to do with the world more generally.[10] Thus, that Ingram identifies the bearer of the past-directed property in the case of grounding (P1) as the haecceity of Socrates is, *prima facie*, a strength of his view *vis-à-vis* other Lucretian views.

Ingram considers proposition (P4) in his discussion of how a Thisness Presentist might ground past truths:

(P4) <Boudica was fierce.>

Ingram wants to ground the truth of (P4) in the fact that Boudica's haecceity currently has a past-directed property, *having been the thisness of a fierce woman*. But of course there are other haecceities around that also were instantiated by fierce women. Take Eleanor Roosevelt's haecceity– it too has the property *having been the thisness of a fierce woman*. Why doesn't Ingram want to locate the ground for (P4) in Eleanor Roosevelt's haecceity having this property? After all, it satisfies the same stated description as that Ingram cites for his preferred ground for (P4). It is important to Ingram that for the purposes of grounding the truth of (P4), the haecceity in question that bears the past-directed property be *Boudica's* haecceity. It is this fact, as we just noted, that allows him to do better than the standard Lucretian presentist who grounds past truths in the world's having various properties: Ingram is able to say that the ground for (P4) has something to do with (P4) in a way that other potential present grounds do not.

Call Boudica's haecceity *B* and Eleanor Roosevelt's haecceity *E*. The ground for the truth of (P4) should involve *B* and not *E*, Ingram contends. Thus, we may see that grounding the truth of (P4) requires more than that

B have the property *having been the thisness of a fierce woman*. Rather, *B* must also stand in the *is the haecceity of* relation to Boudica. It is important for Ingram's account that we ground the truth of (P4) in *Boudica's* haecceity; (P4) is a singular proposition about *Boudica*.

However, that this relation needs to hold between present haecceity *B* and past Boudica is a problem for Ingram. As we saw in the last section, Ingram adopts serious presentism. Thus, present objects can't stand in relations to wholly past objects. Thus, *B* can't stand in the *is the haecceity of* relation to Boudica. Thus, there is a problem with Ingram's own distinctive Lucretianism.

I imagine two replies that Ingram might make to this problem. First, can't we stipulate that it is a primitive fact that *B* is Boudica's haecceity, and *E* Eleanor Roosevelt's? Why does the *is the haecceity of* relation need to hold between a present haecceity and a past object?

Suppose we are constituents about haecceities. Then, it's really difficult to see how *B* could be Boudica's haecceity without *B* standing in the *is the haecceity of* relation to Boudica. After all, Boudica is a constituent of *B*. Suppose, however, that like Ingram we are primitivists about haecceities. Then *B* has no structure with constituents or the like; in such a case, there may not seem to be such an obvious need for the *is the haecceity of* relation to hold between present haecceity and past person. Nevertheless, it seems really unmotivated and *ad hoc* to stipulate that *B* has the property *being the haecceity of Boudica* without the requisite *is the haecceity of* relation holding between *B* and Boudica.[11] How could it be that *B* has the property *being the haecceity of Boudica* without the *is the haecceity of* relation holding between Boudica and *B*?

I imagine a second reply on behalf of Ingram. Suppose that Ingram gave up serious presentism and allowed the requisite troublesome relation to hold between Boudica and *B*. This would be to adopt a form of independence actualism on which objects that don't exist are able to exemplify properties and stand in relations. Once one allows this, however, why not expand the class of relations that objects that don't exist may stand in to do the grounding work the presentist needs to be done?[12] For instance, consider again (P3):

(P3) <World War II occurred after World War I.>

Consider how an eternalist might explain the truth of (P3): World War I and World War II are concrete events that occupy regions of spacetime, and the region of spacetime that World War II occupies is later than the region of spacetime that World War I occupies.[13] Now, for the presentist, neither concrete World War I nor concrete World War II exists. But if objects that don't exist may stand in relations, then World War II may stand in the same *later than* relation to World War I that the eternalist says that they stand in.

Similarly, consider the proposition that Ingram uses to motivate his Thisness Presentist response:

(P4) <Boudica was fierce.>

For the eternalist, Boudica exists in order to be a constituent of (P4); that is, because Boudica exists, she can stand in the *is a constituent of* relation to (P4). Once one gives up serious presentism and adopts a sufficiently robust independence actualism, the presentist may say the same sort of thing.[14] Though Boudica doesn't exist, Boudica may stand in relations. In particular, she may in the *is a constituent of* relation to (P3).

On neither of these independence actualist solutions have we eliminated tense in the way an eternalist would. For instance, (P4) is true because the individual who is a constituent of (P4) WAS fierce. But this is as it should be for a presentist! For a presentist, tense is an ineliminable feature of reality. What we *have* eliminated is the giving of truth conditions in a roundabout Lucretian manner. Ingram's truth conditions may be less roundabout than standard Lucretianism, but they're still roundabout. If we're already allowing objects that don't exist to stand in relations, why not eschew any whiff of Lucretianism?

One advantage to adopting this sort of independence actualism is that it allows one to avoid what I have called "the shifting truthmakers objection" (Davidson [44]). Consider another proposition

(P5) <Boudica is fierce.>

The eternalist is able to say that the ground for both (P4) and (P5) is Boudica's having a property. For the eternalist, the ground for the propositions doesn't shift as time progresses. However, for most presentists, the nature of the grounds for these propositions *does* shift. The ground for (P5) involves Boudica's having a property. The ground for (P4) involves something very different: e.g., the world's having a past-directed property, an haecceity having a past-directed property, or abstract times representing reality in a particular way. That independence actualism allows one to avoid the shifting truthmakers objection is a strength of the independence actualist theory.

I imagine two objections to the independence actualist proposal. The first objection is that independence actualism really is a sort of Meinongianism. But it's not! The Meinongian thinks that in the scope of our widest quantifiers, there are objects that don't exist. The independence actualist denies this. She just denies that property exemplification entails either that the exemplifier exists or is a nonexistent object. In this, the independence actualist takes her motivation from free rather than Meinongian logic.[15]

The second objection is that we are just *stipulating* that the objects that don't exist stand in the requisite relations to do the grounding work we want them to do. How do we know they stand in these relations? In answering this question, it is worth looking at some of the other presentist accounts of grounding past truths. Let's begin first by looking at standard Lucretianism. The most basic description of the standard (Bigelow-type) Lucretian view is something like this: We stipulate that the world has the requisite past-directed properties to ground the propositions about the past that we want to ground. Similarly, if we characterized most simply Ingram's Thisness Presentism's account of grounding past truths, we'd say something like this: Stipulate that currently existing haecceities have the requisite past-directed properties to ground the propositions about the past that we want to ground. Or, if we wanted to characterize the abstract time solution in a very basic way, we'd say something like this: Stipulate that there are abstract times that are analogous to abstract possible worlds, and the abstract times have a primitive ordering relation on them and represent the past accurately so that they are able to ground the past propositions.

Thus, *any* solution to grounding problems for presentism involves some stipulation. Indeed, much metaphysical theorizing involves stipulating entities to solve philosophical problems. Such a stipulation is permissible if it isn't obviously incoherent and solves the philosophical problems one wants to solve. David Lewis famously makes this sort of case for his positing of concrete possible worlds in *On the Plurality of Worlds*:

> Why believe in a plurality of worlds?—Because the hypothesis is serviceable, and that is a reason to think that it is true. The familiar analysis of necessity as truth at all possible worlds was only the beginning. In the last two decades, philosophers have offered a great many more analyses that make reference to possible worlds, or to possible individuals that inhabit possible worlds. I find that record most impressive... (Lewis [82], p. 3).

> If we want the theoretical benefits that talk of [concrete] possibilia brings, the most straightforward way to gain honest title to them is to accept such talk as the literal truth...The benefits are worth their ontological cost. Modal realism is fruitful; that gives us good reason to believe it is true. Good reason; I do not say it is conclusive. Maybe the theoretical benefits to be gained are illusory, because the analyses that use [concrete] possibilia do not succeed on their own terms. Maybe the price is higher than it seems because [Lewis' concretist metaphysics] has unacceptable hidden implications (Lewis [82], p. 4).

Ingram himself points to this sort of Lewisian thinking to justify accepting his Thisness Presentistic grounding of past truths.

In a book on haecceity, I do not have the space to consider the coherence of a metaphysics that allows objects that don't exist to stand in relations, though I have done this elsewhere (Davidson [47]). But we have seen that in order for Ingram's own account of presentist grounding to fare better than ordinary Lucretianism, he will need to allow objects that don't exist to stand in relations. Once one does that, however, why not posit the requisite standing relations to solve the grounding problems one wants to solve, without taking a detour through Lucretianism?

7.3 Application 3: Presentism and Passage

Ingram also thinks that Thisness Presentism may help to explain temporal passage for a presentist. He approaches this topic by way of considering an argument against presentism from a recent paper by Lisa Leininger ([81]). We will work our way to Ingram's application of haecceities to the problem of presentist temporal passage by considering his reply to Leininger's argument. We'll take up her argument first and then see how Ingram marshals the resources of Thisness Presentism in his reply to Leininger. We will close the section by considering first Ingram's reply to Leininger and then the merits of Leininger's argument.

7.3.1 Leininger's Argument Against Presentism

Lisa Leininger gives a complex argument (or perhaps a series of moderately complex arguments, depending on how one individuates arguments) against presentism. I want to set out her argument carefully in this section. In the next section, we will take up Ingram's Thisness Presentist reply to Leininger. After getting clear on Leininger's argument and Ingram's reply, we will consider the merits of each. We will be particularly concerned how haecceities might be brought to bear on the problems that Leininger argues presentism faces.

Leininger argues that there is an incoherence at the heart of presentism. To show this, she begins by characterizing what she argues are two key theses of presentism (Leininger [81], p. 726).

1 *The Present Thesis*: Only the present exists; past and future moments do not exist.
2 *The Change Thesis*: What is present changes; there is a difference in what exists from moment to moment.

Typically, a definition of presentism includes only the Present Thesis. But presentists do certainly think that the Change Thesis is correct, as well. Presentists think that reality is tensed and dynamic. Leininger claims that there is a tension between the two theses: By adopting the Present Thesis, presentists foreclose on the truth of the Change Thesis. The latter Thesis entails, she argues, that there is more than one moment of time, and this contradicts the Present Thesis:

> This means that, for the contents of the present moment to change, there must be a difference in the character of each *successive* present moment. But in order to establish that two successive moments are different, both must exist...
>
> Ultimately, the Change Thesis requires that at least two moments be drawn in the picture of the totality of what exists in the world. On the other hand, the Present Thesis requires that only one moment can be drawn in the picture of the totality of what exists in the world. (Leininger [81], p. 730).

Leininger anticipates a reply from the presentist that involves adopting "surrogates" for non-present moments. These surrogates are the same sorts of entities that the presentist appeals to in replying to grounding concerns (e.g. Lucretian properties or abstract times).

How do we evaluate these surrogates? Leininger claims that any surrogate must be incompatible with a world with only one instant. She then proposes a test to ascertain whether this incompatibility holds.

> [B]ecause temporal change requires a world that is longer than one instant, that by virtue of which temporal change exists (in this case by way of surrogates) must preclude the possibility of a one-instant world...
>
> How does one evaluate whether the presentist's account of temporal change precludes the possibility of a one-instant world? I propose the One Instant Test:
>
> (OIT) Suppose that God creates only this one instant, exactly as it is NOW. Is he able to create-in this one instant-the relevant ingredients by which the presentist establishes temporal change?
>
> If the answer is "No", then the presentist passes the OIT, because that by which the presentist establishes temporal change guarantees a persisting world and so meets a necessary requirement for an adequate account of temporal change. If the answer to the question posed by OIT is "Yes", then the presentist fails the OIT (Leininger [81], p. 732).

Leininger then proceeds to argue that the various surrogates to which the presentist might appeal fail the One Instant Test. That is, the existence of

122 Haecceity Applied

each is consistent with a one-instant world.[16] Let's consider her reasoning around the two surrogates we discussed earlier in the chapter: Lucretian past-directed properties of the sort that Bigelow [17] advocates, and abstract times.

a. Lucretian Properties

Leininger argues that Bigelow-type Lucretian properties as surrogates fail the One Instant Test.

> Consider the OIT: can God create just this one instant and create all of the requisite past-tensed properties in this one instant as well? At first it seems like this cannot be the case. After all, how do these past-tensed properties get created if not by the events (now in the past) that brought them about? This option, however, leads the presentist down an unacceptable path. If the events in the past caused the past-tensed properties to exist in the present, then this causal relation necessitates the existence of the relata–both the past tensed properties and the existence of the past (Leininger [81], p. 733).

Suppose God were to create a one-instant world with all the current past-directed Lucretian properties of the present moment. God's doing this is precluded only if the properties stand in a causal relation to past moments of time. Leininger claims these properties standing in such relations is precluded by presentism (specifically the Present Thesis), as their standing in a causal relation to past moments of time entails that the past moments of time exist.

b. Abstract Times

Leininger argues that abstract times as surrogates (the use of which she calls "ersatz presentism") also fail the One Instant Test.

> [I]n one moment God can create the entirety of the ersatz B-series since the ersatz B-series is merely an abstract object. In this situation, by appealing to the ersatz B-series, it is the case that another moment did exist, even though the world is only one instant in duration. Ersatz presentism fails the OIT: the existence of the ersatz B-series does not necessitate that another moment did exist (Leininger [81], p. 735).[17]

Let's try to summarize the various threads of Leininger's argument. She argues that the Change Thesis entails that there is more than one moment of time, which contradicts the Present Thesis. She imagines the presentist appealing to surrogates to explain how there can be temporal change even though there is only one present moment. To do this work, the surrogates must pass the One Instant Test; that is, their existence must be incompatible with a world in which there is only one instant. All of the surrogates (of which we have examined two) fail the One Instant Test. Therefore, the presentist has no reply to the argument that the Present Thesis is incompatible with the Change Thesis, and the presentist must give up one of these.

Ingram believes that Thisness Presentism offers a way out of these difficulties for the presentist. We turn to his case for this.

7.3.2 Ingram's Thisness Presentist Reply to Leininger

Ingram is sympathetic with much of Leininger's overall argument:

> I agree with Leininger that an account of temporal change must rule out [the possibility of a one-instant world with surrogates] (Ingram [71], p. 160).

> Leininger's argument against surrogates is elegant and compelling. Presentists cannot account for genuine temporal change by posting present surrogates (of past things) because—absent some appropriate development of the presentist metaphysic— the existence of such surrogates does not guarantee that the world persists; the appeal to surrogates is compatible with the possibility of a one-instant world (Ingram [71], p. 161).

Ingram contends that Thisness Presentism may allow the presentist to square the Change and Present Theses. Recall that Ingram wants to ground past facts about the world in presently existing haecceities' having past-directed properties. He argues that such a surrogate passes the One Instant Test:

> The thisness account of temporal change thus precludes the possibility of a one instant world in the following way. If there are uninstantiated thisnesses of past entities, then there must have been a past...Thus, presentists have a way to resolve the incompatibility between the Present Thesis...and the Change Thesis...(Ingram [71], p. 164).

Thus, Ingram contends that the right sort of presentism—Thisness Presentism—allows one to explain how there can be real temporal change in spite of the fact that there is only one moment of time.

7.3.3 Analysis of Leininger's Argument and Ingram's Reply to Leininger

7.3.3.1 Ingram's Reply to Leininger

What should one think of Leininger's complex argument against presentism, and Ingram's Thisness Presentistic reply to Leininger? Let's begin with Ingram's reply before turning to the merits of Leininger's argument. Earlier in the chapter we noted that Ingram's Thisness Presentistic solution to grounding problems really should be thought of as a species of Lucretianism. It is different from Bigelow's [17] well-known formulation of Lucretianism, of course. For Bigelow, the world bears past-directed properties that do work in grounding. For Ingram it is haecceities that bear the past-directed properties. Ingram thinks that his solution is preferable to a view like Bigelow's in that the entity that bears the past-directed properties has something to do with the past proposition it is trying to ground. Even if Ingram were right about this, however, the structure of the two views is importantly similar, and both are properly classed as Lucretian views.

As a Lucretian view, one would expect Ingram's Thisness Presentistic surrogates to stand or fall with the surrogates of the other Lucretian views, and this turns out to be the case. If Leininger's overall argument is sound, it is not enough to point to a surrogate the existence (or exemplification or obtaining) of which entails the existence of a past. Bigelow's (instantiated) past-directed properties entail the existence of a past. Leininger's objection to them is that in order for them to exist there must be a causal relation that holds between the past and the present, and the presentist cannot allow for this (as the instantiation of the relation entails the existence of the relata). The same criticism would hold for Ingram's Thisness Presentism.

If there needs to be a past-present causal relation in order for there to be Bigelow's past-directed properties, the same sort of causal relation would need to hold for Ingram's past-directed properties. If Leininger is right that a presentist can't allow such a relation to hold between past and present moments, Ingram's Thisness Presentistic surrogates would fail alongside Bigelow's Lucretian surrogates. Indeed, Leininger notes exactly this fact in a footnote in which she replies to a referee who suggests a reply like Ingram's:

> [Thisness Presentism], however, encounters a difficultly similar to the difficulty that Bigelow's account faces. Specifically, these haecceities get created by the same events that bring about the existence of their individuals. Thus, there needs to be a causal connection between past events and the presently existing haecceities (Leininger [81], p. 733).

Ingram replies to this footnote by granting that a causal relation holding between a past moment and present moment would be existence-entailing, though denying that the relation that holds between past moments and presently existing haecceities is causal:

> Leininger's claim that "there needs to be a causal connection" between [an entity] x and [its haecceity] T is false...The connection between x and T is not the troublesome existence-entailing relation of "causal necessitation" that Leininger supposes. And, as I see it, the relevant connection between x and T does not have to persist beyond the initial existence of x (Ingram [71], p. 163).

We don't get from Ingram an explanation of the sort of connection there is between x and T, only that it isn't existence-entailing and doesn't need to span between past and present.

This strikes me as not an adequate reply to Leininger. Surely, there are causal relations that hold between x (or past states of affairs involving x) and T. If she is right to dismiss Bigelow-type Lucretian surrogates for relying on cross-time causal relations, she's also right to reject Ingram-type Lucretian haecceity surrogates for the same reason.

Thus, I don't think that Ingram's stance of accepting the soundness of Leininger's argument against other Lucretian surrogates, yet denying its soundness against his own Thisness Presentistic account of grounding, is tenable. If Ingram wants his own presentism to survive Leininger's attack on presentism, he will have to criticize the fundamentals of her argument. In that spirit, we turn to analysis of Leininger's main argument.

7.3.3.2 Leininger's Argument

It is worth considering the merits of Leininger's argument independent of Ingram's response to it. Does her argument show that there is an incoherence in the heart of presentism? One question one might raise about it is why one should think that there can be temporal change only if there is more than one moment in time. We don't really get a robust argument for it in Leininger. This is striking, for this proposition would be properly taken by the presentist to be a flat-out denial of the presentist metaphysic. Leininger's argument that temporal change requires multiple temporal moments consists primarily of a characterization of a temporal diagram in which there is a single house at a time t1 representing things at a particular moment of time. She says:

> In this case, the resident of presentist world is confined to the house in which he lives, and when he looks out into the neighbourhood he sees no other houses. The resident of the house at t1 is looking at everything that exists—and what exists does

not include any other houses. From his point of view as the only existing house, there are no houses that are created and destroyed, one after another; the only thing that exists is his house. There is no temporal change in this picture.

This means that for the contents of the present moment to change, there must be a difference in the character of each *successive* present moment. But in order to establish that two successive moments are different, both must exist...(Leininger [81], p. 730).

I don't see why the presentist should think that this sort of case establishes that there can't be change without more than one moment existing. The presentist's view *just is* that there is just one moment in time and temporal change occurs as time passes. In the house example, the resident of the house doesn't see other houses. This is analogous to what one would see in terms of past and future concrete moments were presentism true. But the presentist's core claim is that in spite of the absence of past and future, there still is temporal becoming and change. In house terms, at the core of presentism is that in spite of the presence of no other houses, as time passes, the attributes of the house change. Maybe there is a problem with this central part of the presentist's metaphysic. But we don't have any sort of argument for it from Leininger that wouldn't properly be taken by a presentist to be a flat-out denial of the presentist's core theses.

Maybe we could provide such an argument for Leininger, however. Here is one way of putting such an argument that *prima facie* would spell trouble for the presentist. In order for there to be change over time, there must be causal relations that hold between times. For a wall to change from blue to red, there must be causal relations that hold between past moments of time in which the wall is blue and present/future moments of time in which the wall is blue. But the presentist can't account for cross-time causal relations. Thus, there can't be temporal change on a presentist's picture.

This may be the sort of objection to presentism that Leininger ultimately has in mind. Leininger's objections to surrogates—which themselves function as parts of replies to the inconsistency of the Change and Present Theses—are put in terms of the presentist's inability to account for cross-time causal relations. Then, maybe the dialectic of her argument should be understood as follows: The Change Thesis requires cross-time causal relations, which the Present Thesis precludes. Surrogates (e.g. Lucretian properties or abstract times) also require cross-time causal relations and so won't help with the original conflict between the Change Thesis and the Present Thesis.

Haecceity Applied 127

The issue with rendering her argument this way is that we may see that it's another standard sort of objection to presentism from cross-time relations rather than a novel problem for presentism. Accounting for cross-time relations is a serious issue for the presentist (see e.g. Davidson [41], Crisp [35], Ciuni and Torrengo [32] for discussion). But different presentists have mounted various replies to this problem. For instance, one might construe the relata of the causal relation as involving entities that exist at every time (e.g. abstract states of affairs or propositions). Or, one might adopt independence actualism and allow causal relations to hold between past events that don't exist and present events that do exist (Davidson [47], ch. 3). Ingram himself thinks that Thisness Presentism offers him a reply to problems of cross-time relations. He construes the causal relation as holding between tensed properties of haecceities. This is a solution that is functionally similar to that of taking causation to hold between always existing abstract states of affairs.

To recap, I don't think that Ingram's reply to Leininger's argument that there is an inconsistency between Change and Present Theses works. Or more precisely, I don't think Ingram's reply works any better than a Bigelow-type Lucretian surrogate reply works, and Ingram himself thinks that a Bigelow-type Lucretian surrogate reply to Leininger fails. Nevertheless, I don't think that Leininger's argument is convincing. There is no convincing argument in her paper for the necessity of multiple existing concrete times for the truth of the Change Thesis. We might supply to her an argument for this based on cross-time relations. Then, of course, we would see the Leininger argument as another argument against presentism from cross-time causal relations, and the standard presentist replies to these sorts of concerns would apply to her argument.

Notes

1 He explicitly takes his ontology of haecceity from Robert Adams ([6]). One might wonder whether on this sort of metaphysic an haecceity could be destroyed by God. After all, for Ingram an haecceity is a contingent existent; and other contingent existences can be destroyed by God.
2 This solution isn't new (see e.g. Davidson [41], Keller [76]), though Ingram's might be the most thorough defense of it.
3 See Davidson [47], ch. 3 for more on this.
4 I should note that Ingram explicitly is a serious actualist. He appeals to "serious actualism" as the principle that allows him to reject a solution like that of (1) (Ingram [71], p. 86). But it is really serious *presentism* that he needs here. Thus, we will take him to be a serious presentist, in addition to a serious actualist.
5 Presumably, another reason to accept structured propositions is that they allow one to account for how the meaning of an entire sentence is a function of the meanings of the parts of the sentence.

128 Haecceity Applied

6 Though I have defended a version of (1) over alternatives for similar sorts of problems in my [47], ch. 3.
7 Or more precisely, "Socrates was a philosopher" would express a proposition with Socrates as a constituent.
8 I talk more about such issues in (Davidson [47], ch. 5).
9 See, e.g. Caplan and Sanson [23] and Davidson [44] for discussion.
10 See e.g. Merricks [95], pp. 133 ff.; and Ingram [71], pp. 109–110 for discussion of this sort of objection.
11 I talk some about this with "the relational properties solution" in Davidson [41].
12 I consider how independence actualism may help the presentist in replying to objections to presentism in Davidson [47], ch. 3.
13 I'm not here saying that the eternalist will think that there is any fundamental metaphysical difference between the two regions. But even an eternalist will accept an arrow of time that is tied to causation and thermodynamics.
14 Thus obviating the need for haecceities as constituents of singular propositions.
15 I discuss the difference between independence actualism and Meinongianism, as well as the difference between free and Meinongian logics in Davidson [47], ch. 1.
16 It's worth noting that the various surrogates to which presentists might appeal generally are taken to be abstract necessary existents. So, properly, the question is whether the instantiation/exemplification/obtaining of the surrogate is compatible with a one-instant world.
17 Again, it's not clear that the presentist will want to say that God can *create* the entire series of abstract times. She may just want to say that God can make them represent the world in a certain way (in terms of ordering and which represent the things that occur in the world).

Epilogue

In this book, we have considered various issues in the metaphysics and epistemology of haecceity. In Chapter 1, we surveyed historical thinking about haecceity, from John Duns Scotus in the late 13th and early 14th centuries to Gary Rosenkrantz at the end of the 20th century. In Chapter 2, we considered three views as to the nature of haecceity, namely, partism, primitivism, and constituentism. There I defended a type of constituentism, *sui generis* constituentism. In Chapter 3, we examined various arguments for and against the existence of haecceities. There I argued that the best-known arguments for haecceities, *individuative arguments*, are not successful in establishing the existence of haecceities. *Semantic arguments*, however, are successful in showing that there are haecceities. I argued further that there are no compelling arguments against the existence of haecceities. Thus, I concluded, we have *prima facie* reason to think that there are haecceities.

In Chapter 4, we considered different conceptions of the qualitative-quidditative distinction. I argued that *quidditative constituentism*—that quidditative properties have individuals that exemplify them as constituents—is the best way to mark the distinction between qualitative and quidditative properties. In Chapter 5, I argued that none of the arguments that there can't be unexemplified haecceities succeeds. Furthermore, there are promising arguments that there can be unexemplified haecceities. Thus, I concluded that we have a *prima facie* case for believing in unexemplified haecceities.

In Chapter 6, we considered our ability to grasp haecceities. We examined an argument from Gary Rosenkrantz that we aren't able to grasp haecceities of ordinary objects in our environment, and an argument from Jonathan Kvanvig that we can. I concluded that Rosenkrantz's argument that we can't grasp haecceities of ordinary objects fails, and Kvanvig's argument (which was leveled against the primitivist Chisholm) misses its stated mark. I argued further that the constituentist about haecceity has a ready explanation as to how we may grasp all sorts of haecceities. This salutary effect on our epistemic grasp of haecceities is a further strength of constituentism. Thus, I maintain that we should think that our ability to grasp haecceities is wide-ranging.

In the last chapter, we considered a recent application of the metaphysics of haecceities, what David Ingram calls "Thisness Presentism." We saw there three things: how haecceities may serve as constituents of singular propositions, how haecceities may be used to help the presentist with problems with grounding truths about the past, and how haecceities may help the presentist try to explain temporal passage. Ultimately, Ingram's application of Thisness Presentism doesn't improve upon extant solutions to these problems. But it does show how one might try to use haecceities to solve longstanding problems in the metaphysics of time.

I view this book as a start of a metaphysical project, rather than the last word in one. There is, no doubt, much more to be said in future work about the various topics in this book. I hope that this book proves useful as an impetus to such work.

Bibliography

1. Marilyn McCord Adams. Ockham on Identity and Distinction. *Franciscan Studies*, 36(1):5–74, 1976.
2. Marilyn McCord Adams. *William Ockham*. University of Notre Dame Press, Notre Dame, 1987.
3. Robert Merrihew Adams. Theories of Actuality. In Michael J. Loux, editor, *The Possible and the Actual: Readings in the Metaphysics of Modality*, pp. 190–210. Cornell University Press, Ithaca, 1974.
4. Robert Merrihew Adams. Primitive Thisness and Primitive Identity. *Journal of Philosophy*, 76(1):5–26, 1979.
5. Robert Merrihew Adams. Actualism and Thisness. *Synthese*, 49(1):3–41, 1981.
6. Robert Merrihew Adams. Time and Thisness. *Midwest Studies in Philosophy*, 11(1):315–329, 1986.
7. Robert Merrihew Adams. Thisness and Time Travel. *Philosophia*, 25(1–4):407–415, 1997.
8. Robert Merrihew Adams. *What Is, and What Is in Itself*. Oxford University Press, Oxford, 2021.
9. Robert Almeder. Peirce's Pragmatism and Scotistic Realism. *Transactions of the Charles S. Peirce Society*, 9(1):3–23, 1973.
10. Robert R. Andrews. Haecceity in the Metaphysics of John Duns Scotus. In *Johannes Duns Scotus 1308–2008*, in Archa Verbi/Subsidia, 5:151—61, 2010.
11. D. M. Armstrong. *A World of States of Affairs*. Cambridge University Press, New York, 1997.
12. Andrew M. Bailey. No Bare Particulars. *Philosophical Studies*, 158(1):31–41, 2012.
13. Todd Bates. *Duns Scotus and the Problem of Universals*. Continuum, New York, 2010.

14 Gustav Bergmann. *Realism: A Critique of Brentano and Meinong*. University of Wisconsin Press, Madison, 1967.

15 Michael Bergmann. A New Argument from Actualism to Serious Actualism. *Noûs*, 30(3):356–359, 1996.

16 George Berkeley. *Principles of Human Knowledge and Three Dialogues*. Oxford University Press, Oxford, 2009.

17 John Bigelow. Presentism and Properties. *Philosophical Perspectives*, 10:35–52, 1996.

18 Max Black. The Identity of Indiscernables. *Mind*, 61(242):153–164, 1952.

19 John F. Boler. *Charles Peirce and Scholastic Realism*. University of Washington Press, Seattle, 1963.

20 Jason Bowers and Meg Wallace. The Haecceitic Euthyphro Problem. *Analysis*, 78(1):13–22, 2018.

21 David Braun. Empty Names. *Noûs*, 27(4):449–469, 1993.

22 David Braun. Empty Names, Fictional Names, Mythical Names. *Noûs*, 39(4):596–631, 2005.

23 Ben Caplan and David Sanson. The Way Things Were. *Philosophy and Phenomenological Research*, 81(1):24–39, 2010.

24 Chalmers, David. *The Character of Consciousness*. Oxford University Press, Oxford, 2010.

25 Roderick Chisholm. *Person and Object: A Metaphysical Study*. Open Court, La Salle, 1976.

26 Roderick Chisholm. Possibility without Haecceity. In *On Metaphysics*. University of Minnesota Press, Minneapolis, 1989.

27 Roderick M. Chisholm. The Logic of Knowing. *Journal of Philosophy*, 60(25):773–795, 1963.

28 Roderick M. Chisholm. Individuation: Some Thomistic Questions and Answers. *Grazer Philosophische Studien*, 1(1):25–41, 1975.

29 Roderick M. Chisholm. *The First Person: An Essay on Reference and Intentionality*. University of Minnesota Press, Minneapolis, 1981.

30 Roderick M. Chisholm. Events without Times an Essay on Ontology. *Noûs*, 24(3):413–427, 1990.

31 Chisholm, Roderick. Objects and Persons: Revisions and Replies. In Ernest Sosa, editor, *Essays on the Philosophy of Roderick Chisholm*, pp. 317–388. Rodopi, Amsterdam, 1979.

32 Roberto Ciuni and Giuliano Torrengo. Presentism and Cross-temporal Relations. In Roberto Ciuni, Giuliano Torrengo, and Kristie Miller,

editors, *New Papers on the Present: Focus on Presentism*, New Papers on the Present: Focus on Presentism, pp. 153–172. Verlag, Munich, 2013.

33 J.A. Cover and O'Leary-Hawthorne, John. *Substance and Individuation in Leibniz*. Cambridge University Press, Cambridge, 1999.

34 Sam Cowling. Non-qualitative Properties. *Erkenntnis*, 80(2):275–301, 2015.

35 Thomas M. Crisp. Presentism and "Cross-time" Relations. *American Philosophical Quarterly*, 42(1):5–17, 2005.

36 Chris Daly. Tropes. *Proceedings of the Aristotelian Society*, 94(1):253–262, 1994.

37 Chris Daly. Scepticism about Grounding. In Fabrice Correia and Benjamin Schnieder, editors, *Metaphysical Grounding: Understanding the Structure of Reality*. Cambridge University Press, Cambridge, 2012.

38 Chris Daly. Explanation Good, Grounding Bad. *The Monist*, 103(6):270–286, 2023.

39 Matthew Davidson. Direct Reference and Singular Propositions. *American Philosophical Quarterly*, 37(3):285–300, 2000.

40 Matthew Davidson. Introduction. In Matthew Davidson, editor, *Essays in the Metaphysics of Modality by Alvin Plantinga*. Oxford University Press, New York, 2003.

41 Matthew Davidson. Presentism and the Non-Present. *Philosophical Studies*, 113(1):77–92, 2003.

42 Matthew Davidson, editor. *On Sense and Direct Reference*. McGraw Hill, New York, 2007.

43 Matthew Davidson. Transworld Identity, Singular Propositions, and Picture Thinking. In Matthew Davidson, editor, *On Sense and Direct Reference*, pp. 559–568. McGraw-Hill, New York, 2007.

44 Matthew Davidson. Presentism and Grounding Past Truths. In Roberto Ciuni, Giuliano Torrengo, and Kristie Miller, editors, *New Papers on the Present: Focus on Presentism*, pp. 153–172. Verlag, Munich, 2013.

45 Matthew Davidson. The Logical Space of Social Trinitarianism. *Faith and Philosophy*, 33(3):333–357, 2016.

46 Matthew Davidson. Putting the Ghost Back in the Machine: An Exploration of Somatic Dualism. *Pacific Philosophical Quarterly*, 100(2):624–641, 2019.

47 Matthew Davidson. *The Metaphysics of Existence and Nonexistence: Actualism, Meinongianism, and Predication*. Bloomsbury, London, 2023.

48 Jeffrey R. Di Leo. Peirce's Haecceitism. *Transactions of the Charles S. Peirce Society*, 27(1):79–109, 1991.
49 Joseph Diekemper. Thisness and Events. *Journal of Philosophy*, 106(5):255–276, 2009.
50 Joseph Diekemper. The Ontology of Thisness. *Philosophy and Phenomenological Research*, 90(1):49–71, 2015.
51 T. Scott Dixon. Plural Slot Theory. In Karen Bennett and Dean Zimmerman, editors, *Oxford Studies in Metaphysics Volume 11*, pp. 193–223. Oxford University Press, Oxford, 2018.
52 Kit Fine. Plantinga on the Reduction of Possibilist Discourse. In James Tomberlin and Peter van Inwagen, editors, *Alvin Plantinga*, pp. 145–186. Springer, Dordrecht, 1985.
53 Kit Fine. Neutral Relations. *Philosophical Review*, 109(1):1–33, 2000.
54 Alfred J. Freddoso. Review of Suarez on Individuation, Metaphysical Disputation V: Individual Unity and Its Principle by Jorge J. E. Gracia. *Philosophy and Phenomenological Research*, 44(3):419–421, 1984.
55 Peter Fritz. Being Somehow without (Possibly) Being Something. *Mind*, 132(526):348–371, 2023.
56 Peter Fritz and Jeremy Goodman. Higher-Order Contingentism, Part 1: Closure and Generation. *Journal of Philosophical Logic*, 45(6):645–695, 2016.
57 Daniel Garber. Leibniz on Form and Matter. *Early Science and Medicine*, 2(3):326–351, 1997.
58 Hester Goodenough Gelber. *Logic and the Trinity: A Clash of Values in Scholastic Thought, 1300–1335*. Ph.D. Dissertation, University of Wisconsin.
59 Cody Gilmore. Slots in Universals. *Oxford Studies in Metaphysics*, 8:187–233, 2013.
60 Jorge J.E. Gracia. Introduction: The Problem of Individuation. In Jorge J.E. Gracia, editor, *Individuation in Scholasticism: The Later Middle Ages and the Counter Reformation: 1150–1650*, pp. 1–21. SUNY, Albany, 1994.
61 Maurice J. O.F.M Grajewski. *The Formal Distinction of Duns Scotus: A Study in Metaphysics*. Ph.D. Dissertation, Catholic University of America.
62 Ian Hacking. The Identity of Indiscernibles. *Journal of Philosophy*, 72(9):249–256, 1975.
63 Katherine Hawley. Identity and Indiscernibility. *Mind*, 118(469):101–119, 2009.

Bibliography

64 John Hawthorne. Identity. In Michael J. Loux and Dean W. Zimmerman, editors, *The Oxford Handbook of Metaphysics*, pp. 99–130. Oxford University Press, Oxford, 2003.

65 Desmond Paul Henry. Ockham and the Formal Distinction. *Franciscan Studies*, 25:285–292, 1965.

66 Vera Hoffmann-Kolss. Defining Qualitative Properties. *Erkenntnis*, 84(5):995–1010, 2019.

67 Thomas Hofweber. Ambitious, Yet Modest Metaphysics. In Ryan Wasserman David Chalmers, David Manley, editor, *Metametaphysics: New Essays in the Foundations of Ontology*, pp. 260–289. Oxford University Press, Oxford, 2009.

68 Arthur Hyman and James J. Walsh, editors. *Philosophy in the Middle Ages (Second Edition): The Christian, Islamic, and Jewish Traditions*. Hackett, Indianapolis, 1983.

69 David Ingram. The Virtues of Thisness Presentism. *Philosophical Studies*, 173(11):2867–2888, 2016. https://doi.org/10.1007/s11098-016-0641-3

70 David Ingram. Thisnesses, Propositions, and Truth. *Pacific Philosophical Quarterly*, 99(3):442–463, 2018.

71 David Ingram. *Thisness Presentism: An Essay on Time, Truth, and Ontology*. Routledge, London, 2019.

72 Jackson, Frank. *From Metaphysics to Ethics: A Defence of Conceptual Analysis*. Oxford University Press, Oxford, 1998.

73 Thomas Jager. An Actualistic Semantics for Quantified Modal Logic. *Notre Dame Journal of Formal Logic*, 23(3):335–349, 1982.

74 Michael Joseph Jordan. *Duns Scotus on the Formal Distinction*. Ph.D. Dissertation, Rutgers University.

75 David Kaplan. How to Russell a Frege-Church. *Journal of Philosophy*, 72(19):716–729, 1975.

76 Simon Keller. Presentism and Truthmaking. In Dean Zimmerman, editor, *Oxford Studies in Metaphysics, Vol. 1*, pp. 83–104. Oxford University Press, Oxford, 2004.

77 E. J. Khamara. Indiscernables and the Absolute Theory of Space and Time. *Studia Leibnitiana*, 20(2):140–159, 1988.

78 Peter King. Duns Scotus on the Common Nature and the Individual Differentia. *Philosophical Topics*, 20(2):51–76, 1992.

79 Gottfried Wilhelm Leibniz. *Leibniz: New Essays on Human Understanding*. Cambridge University Press, Cambridge, 1996.

80 Gottfried Wilhelm Leibniz and Samuel Clarke. *Leibniz and Clarke: Correspondence*. Hackett Publishing Company, Indianapolis, 2000.

81 Lisa Leininger. Presentism and the Myth of Passage. *Australasian Journal of Philosophy*, 93(4):724–739, 2015.

82 David Lewis. *On the Plurality of Worlds*. Wiley-Blackwell, Oxford, 1986.

83 Bernard Linsky and Edward N. Zalta. In Defense of the Simplest Quantified Modal Logic. *Philosophical Perspectives*, 8:431–458, 1994.

84 Michael Lockwood. On Predicating Proper Names. *Philosophical Review*, 84(4):471–498, 1975.

85 Michael J. Loux. *Substance and Attribute a Study in Ontology*. Springer, Dordrecht, 1978.

86 E. J. Lowe. Review: Haecceity: An Ontological Essay. *Mind*, 104(413):202–205, 1995.

87 E. J. Lowe. Individuation. In Michael J. Loux and Dean W. Zimmerman, editors, *The Oxford Handbook of Metaphysics*. Oxford University Press, Oxford, 2003.

88 Peter Ludlow and Norah Martin, editors. *Externalism and Self-Knowledge*. CSLI, Stanford, 1998.

89 Gottfried Martin. *Leibniz: Logic and Metaphysics*. Barnes and Noble, New York, 1964.

90 A.A. Maurer. *The Philosophy of William of Ockham in the Light of Its Principles*. Pontifical Institute of Mediaeval Studies, Toronto, 1999.

91 McCullough, Laurence B. *Leibniz on Individuals and Individuation*. Springer, Dordrecht, 1996.

92 Alan McMichael. A Problem for Actualism About Possible Worlds. *The Philosophical Review*, 92(1):49–66, 1983.

93 Christopher Menzel. Actualism, Ontological Commitment, and Possible World Semantics. *Synthese*, 85(3):355–389, 1990.

94 Christopher Menzel. The True Modal Logic. *Journal of Philosophical Logic*, 20(4):331–374, 1991.

95 Trenton Merricks. *Truth and Ontology*. Oxford University Press, Oxford, 2007.

96 Trenton Merricks. *Propositions*. Oxford University Press, Oxford, 2015.

97 W. Ockham, P. Boehner, and S.F. Brown, editors. *Ockham: Philosophical Writings: A Selection*. Hackett Classics Series. Hackett, 1990.

98 Woosuk Park. Haecceitas and the Bare Particular. *Review of Metaphysics*, 44(2):375 – 397, 1990.
99 Charles Parsons. Platonism and Mathematical Intuition in Kurt Godel's Thought. *Bulletin of Symbolic Logic*, 1(1):44–74, 1995.
100 Charles S. Peirce. *Collected Papers of Charles Sanders Peirce*. Harvard University Press, Cambridge, 1931.
101 Alvin Plantinga. *The Nature of Necessity*. Oxford University Press, Oxford, 1974.
102 Alvin Plantinga. De Essentia. *Grazer Philosophische Studien*, 7(1):101–121, 1979.
103 Alvin Plantinga. Replies to my Colleagues. In James Tomberlin, editor, *Alvin Plantinga*, pp. 313–396. Springer Netherlands, Dordrecht, 1985.
104 Alvin Plantinga. Self-Profile. In James Tomberlin, editor, *Alvin Plantinga*, pp. 3–97. Springer Netherlands, Dordrecht, 1985.
105 Alvin Plantinga. Actualism and Possible Worlds. In Matthew Davidson, editor, *Essays in the Metaphysics of Modality*, pp. 103–122. Oxford, New York, 2003.
106 Alvin Plantinga. The Boethian Compromise. In Matthew Davidson, editor, *Essays in the Metaphysics of Modality*, pp. 122–139. Oxford University Press, New York, 2003.
107 Alvin Plantinga. De Essentia. In Matthew Davidson, editor, *Essays in the Metaphysics of Modality*, pp. 139–158. Oxford University Press, New York, 2003.
108 Alvin Plantinga. *Essays in the Metaphysics of Modality*. Oxford University Press, New York, 2003.
109 Alvin Plantinga. On Existentialism. In Matthew Davidson, editor, *Essays in the Metaphysics of Modality*, pp. 158–176. Oxford University Press, New York, 2003.
110 Plantinga, Alvin. World and Essence. In Matthew Davidson, editor, *Essays in the Metaphysics of Modality*, pp. 46–72. Oxford University Press, New York, 2003.
111 John L. Pollock. *The Foundations of Philosophical Semantics*. Princeton University Press, Princeton, 1984.
112 John L. Pollock. Plantinga on Possible Worlds. In James Tomberlin, editor, *Alvin Plantinga*, pages 121–144. Springer Netherlands, Dordrecht, 1985.
113 A. N. Prior. The Possibly-True and the Possible. In Anthony Kenny and Geach, P.T., editors, *Papers in Logic and Ethics*, pages 187–202. Massachusetts, Amherst, 1976.

114 A. N. Prior and Kit Fine. *Worlds, Times, and Selves*. Massachussetts, Amherst, 1977.

115 Alan R. Rhoda. Presentism, Truthmakers, and God. *Pacific Philosophical Quarterly*, 90(1):41–62, 2009.

116 Gary S. Rosenkrantz. The Pure and the Impure. *Logique Et Analyse*, 22(88):515, 1979.

117 Gary S. Rosenkrantz. *Haecceity: An Ontological Essay*. Springer, Dordrecht, 1993.

118 Ross, James F. Introduction. In *Francisco Suarez: On Formal and Universal Unity*, pp. 1–28. Marquette University Press, Milwaukee, 1965.

119 Nathan Salmon. *Reference and Essence*. Princeton University Press, Princeton, 1981.

120 Nathan Salmon. *Frege's Puzzle*. Ridgeview, Atascadero, 1986.

121 Nathan Salmon. Existence. *Philosophical Perspectives*, 1:49–108, 1987.

122 Stephen Schiffer. *The Things We Mean*. Oxford University Press, Oxford, 2003.

123 Theodore Sider. Bare Particulars. *Philosophical Perspectives*, 20(1):387–397, 2006.

124 Alexander Skiles. There Is No Haecceitic Euthyphro Problem. *Analysis*, 79(3):477–484, 2019.

125 Scott Soames. *Beyond Rigidity: The Unfinished Semantic Agenda of Naming and Necessity*. Oxford University Press, Oxford, 2002.

126 Paul Vincent Spade, editor. *Five Texts on the Mediaeval Problem of Universals*. Hackett, Indianapolis, 1994.

127 Jeff Speaks. On Possibly Nonexistent Propositions. *Philosophy and Phenomenological Research*, 85(3):528–562, 2012.

128 Robert Stalnaker. Merely Possible Propositions. In Bob and Hoffman Hale, editor, *Modality: Metaphysics, Logic, and Epistemology*, pp. 21–33. Oxford University Press, Oxford, 2010.

129 Robert Stalnaker. *Mere Possibilities Metaphysical Foundations of Modal Semantics*. Princeton University Press, Princeton, 2012.

130 Francisco Suárez. *Metaphysical Disputation V: Individual Unity and Its Principle*. Marquette University Press, Milwaukee, 1982.

131 Amie L. Thomasson. *Fiction and Metaphysics*. Cambridge University Press, Cambridge, 1998.

132 Amie L. Thomasson. *Ontology Made Easy*. Oxford University Press, Oxford, 2014.

133 John A. Trentman. Scholasticism in the Seventeenth Century. In Norman Kretzmann, Anthony Kenny, Jan Pinborg, and Eleonore Stump, editors, *The Cambridge History of Later Medieval Philosophy: From the Rediscovery of Aristotle to the Disintegration of Scholasticism, 1100–1600*, pp. 818–837. Cambridge University Press, Cambridge, 1982.

134 Jason Turner. Strong and Weak Possibility. *Philosophical Studies*, 125(2):191–217, 2005.

135 James Van Cleve. There Are No Necessary Connections between Distinct Existences. *Oxford Studies in Metaphysics*, (forthcoming).

136 Peter van Inwagen. Creatures of Fiction. *American Philosophical Quarterly*, 14(4):299–308, 1977.

137 Peter van Inwagen. The Doctrine of Arbitrary Undetached Parts. *Pacific Philosophical Quarterly*, 62(2):123–137, 1981.

138 Peter Van Inwagen. *Existence: Essays in Ontology*. Cambridge University Press, Cambridge, 2014.

139 Vier, Peter C. *Evidence and Its Function According to John Duns Scotus*. Franciscian Institute, St. Bonaventure, 1951.

140 Edward J. Wierenga. *The Nature of God: An Inquiry into Divine Attributes*. Cornell University Press, Ithaca, 1989.

141 Timothy Williamson. *Modal Logic as Metaphysics*. Oxford University Press, Oxford, 2013.

142 Allan B. Wolter. John Duns Scotus. In Jorge J. E. Gracia, editor, *Individuation in Scholasticism: The Later Middle Ages and the Counter-Reformation, 1150–1650*, pp. 217–299. State University of New York Press, Albany, 1994.

Index

A
abstract times 115
actualism 62–63, 86
Adams, Robert 1, 5, 23–24, 30, 37, 45–56, 60, 71, 75, 78, 90, 96, 113, 115
argument from reidentification 104–107
arguments against haecceity 64–71
arguments for haecceity, individuative 43–60
arguments for haecceity, semantic 60–63
Aristotle 8
Avicenna 6, 9

B
Bergmann, Michael 94
Bigelow, John 115, 119, 122, 124, 127
Black, Max 23, 45, 64–65
Bowers, Jason 69–71
Braun, David 40, 110

C
Chalmers, David 85
Chisholm, Roderick 3, 21, 22, 29, 30, 34, 37, 60, 66–68, 100, 102–105, 115
Ciuni, Roberto 127
common nature 6
constituentism 1, 28, 35–42, 66–69, 95–96, 100, 104, 107, 117

constituentism, slot-theoretic 30, 31, 37, 40–42, 68
constituentism, *sui generis* 30, 31, 37, 40–42, 68
Cowling, Sam 36, 84
Crisp, Thomas 115, 127

D
Daly, Chris 33, 42, 73
Di Leo, Jeffrey R. 18
Diekemper, Joseph 30, 53–57, 60
direct reference 61, 83, 113–114
distinction, formal 7
distinction, mental 7
distinction, real 7
Dixon, Scott 31, 41

E
eternalism 48
existentialism 87

F
Fine, Kit 31, 41, 90
Freddoso, Alfred 13
Fregean semantics 114
Fritz, Peter 99

G
Gilmore, Cody 31
Gödel, Kurt 101
Goodman, Jeremy 99
Gracia, Jorge J.E. 12, 13

H

haecceitism 3, 4, 27, 51, 69–71
Hawley, Katherine 76
Hawthorne, John 75, 84
Henry of Ghent 8
Hoffman-Kolss, Vera 80–82
Hofweber, Thomas 73

I

independence actualism 40, 84, 87, 88, 95, 97, 99, 110, 117–119, 127
Ingram, David 3, 30, 77–78, 109–127

J

Jackson, Frank 85
Jager, Thomas 63, 97–98

K

Kant, Immanuel 45
Kaplan, David 113
Khamara, Edward J. 80, 84
King, Peter 7
Kripke, Saul 62–63
Kvanvig, Jonathan 100, 102–104

L

Leibniz, G.W. 5, 10, 14–17
Leininger, Lisa 120–127
Lewis, David 119–120
Locke, John 32, 33, 34
Lockwood, Michael 60
Loux, Michael 67–68, 79–80
Lowe, E.J. 65, 69
Lucretianism 115–118, 122–124, 127

M

McMichael, Alan 63, 87, 97–98
Meinongianism 84
Menzel, Christopher 63, 87, 90, 98
Merricks, Trenton 61, 88, 111, 115

N

nature, common 7

necessitism 89, 113
negative existentials 114

O

Ockham, William 8, 11, 12, 13, 44, 46, 49–53, 57, 59, 69

P

Park, Woosuk 65
Parsons, Terrence 107
partism 1, 28–30, 32–35, 68
partism, hylomorphic 28–29, 32, 100
partism, non-hylomorphic 28–29, 32
Peirce, C.S. 5, 18–20
Plantinga, Alvin 20, 22, 23, 24, 30, 35, 36, 60–63, 74, 75, 78, 85, 89–94, 112, 115
Pollock, John 90
presentism 48, 109–127
primitivism 1, 28, 30, 35–42, 66, 68, 100, 104, 107, 109, 117
Prior, Arthur 89
properties, qualitative 2, 35, 36, 74–84
properties, quidditative 2, 35–36, 74–84
properties, world-indexed 20

Q

quidditative constituentism 2, 74, 83–84

R

Rosenkrantz, Gary 1, 2, 3, 5, 24, 25, 30, 37, 57–60, 69, 75, 76, 100, 102, 105–108

S

Salmon, Nathan 30, 38, 40, 99, 113
Schiffer, Stephen 72
Scotus, John Duns 1, 5, 6, 9, 12, 13, 19, 28, 29, 44, 105–108
semantic externalism 49, 50
serious actualism 88, 111, 112
serious presentism 111, 116–117

shifting truthmakers objection 118–119
Sider, Theodore 65
singular propositions 36, 37, 38, 60, 89, 94–95, 109–114
Skiles, Alexander 73
Soames, Scott 40
Speaks, Jeff 93–94
Stalnaker, Robert 90, 91
Suárez, Francisco 10, 12, 13, 14
substance 32, 33, 34, 65–66

T
Thisness Presentism 109–127
Thomasson, Amie 40, 72

Torrengo, Giuliano 127
tropes 29, 32, 34
truth, inside/outside a world 77, 84, 90–91, 114
Turner, Jason 92–93

V
Van Cleve, James 42
van Inwagen, Peter 29, 34, 40, 62
Vier, Peter C. 105, 108

W
Wallace, Meg 69–71
Wierenga, Edward 24, 100
Williamson, Timothy 89, 99, 113